The Art of Poetry volume 5

Love Through the Ages, *post-1900 poems*

Published by Peripeteia Press Ltd.

First published September 2016

ISBN: 978-0-9954671-0-1

Peripeteia.webs.com

Contents

General Introduction to the The Art of Poetry series

The philosopher Nietzsche described his work as 'the greatest gift that [mankind] has ever been given'. The Elizabethan poet Edmund Spenser hoped his book **The Faerie Queene** would transform its readers into noblemen. In comparison, our aims for *The Art of Poetry* series of books are a little more modest. Fundamentally we aim to provide books that will be of maximum use to English students and their teachers. In our experience few students read essays on poetry, yet, whatever specification they are studying, they have to write analytical essays on poetry. So, we've offering some models, written in a lively and accessible style. In Volume 1 we chose canonical poems for a number of reasons: Firstly they are simply great poems, well worth reading and studying; secondly we chose poems from across time so that they sketch in outline major developments in English poetry, from the Elizabethan period up until the present day. And, being canonical poems, they often crop up on GCSE and A-level specifications, so our material will be useful critical accompaniment and revision material. Volumes 2 & 3 focused on modern poems from the *Forward Poems of the Decade* anthology. Our latest offering, volumes 4 & 5 tackle AQA's anthology *Love Through the Ages*.

Introduction to *Volume 5: Love Through the Ages, post-1900 poems*

The theme

According to the Bible it's the greatest of the virtues. According to 'The Beatles' it's all you need. According to Shakespeare it's like a summer's day or a star to navigate by, even during the roughest tempests. And it's also constant, altering not 'when it alteration finds'. Or it's a fever, a madness, a drug, a delirium. Music, apparently is the food of it. And it will always, 'Joy Division' tell us, 'tear us apart, again'.

A shape-shifter, it comes in many various types and guises: Forbidden and illicit; secret and intimate; spiritual and divine; brotherly and platonic; deathless or fatal, filial and patriotic, tender or tempestuous. The Ancient Greeks divided it into four types - *eros* [sexual passion], *agape* [unconditional and spiritual], *philia* [brotherly] and *storge* [empathy]. Surely it is the greatest, most written about subject of them all, greater even than death - love.

But, as the poet W. H. Auden asked 'What is the truth about love?' Does it reside, for instance, in the heart or the head? Is it a universal natural feeling or an abstract concept, malleable to time, place and taste? Is what we call 'love' the same emotion that Shakespeare wrote about? Or has the idea of love changed? Is being in love to be touched by the divine, to be struck by a fatal disease? Or, perhaps, both? At the same time. Is modern love poetry the same as, or different from, earlier poetry in this vein?

AQA's anthology of love poems might help us get a handle on the true nature of love. Herein we have the heat of love as well as the agonies of love, love cooling and hardening into something bitter, or love unrequited, unfulfilled, love cruelly rejected. And secret or transgressive love is here too as well as fatal love, doomed love, love of parents and elegies for lost loves. In a handful of poems, AQA's anthology takes us through many of the antechambers of the human heart.

Why buy this book?

Search the internet and no doubt you'll find essays on most of the poems featured in the AQA anthology. Some of these essays will be good, perhaps great, while others will be moderate or poor or indifferent. Few, if any, however, will have been written expressly for A-level English Literature students and teachers following the AQA specification. Our essays are not designed to provide all the answers, or readings that can simply be learnt and regurgitated in exam conditions. Instead, we aim to demonstrate what happens when sharp critical analysis meets great literary texts. And, we try to express this analysis in a lively, engaging style, tailored specially for A-level students.

To engage in literary criticism is to enter a critical debate. When reading secondary material on a text you're not just looking for material to use, you should be searching for readings you agree with and, crucially, ones with which you disagree. Our essays are designed to inform and stimulate your own reading, to help you refine your own understanding, both of these poems and of what close reading of poetry entails. We hope and expect that sometimes you'll disagree with our interpretations; the experience will help you form your own alternative interpretations and have confidence in them. Our aim is to send you back to the poems with refreshed and renewed interest, so that you will read them more avidly and more expertly. In the end, that is the best way to get the most out of the experience of studying literary texts and of achieving the best results.

Critical methodology

In a recent article for the English & Media Centre blog[1] Barbara Bleiman worried about the quality of poetry criticism she was reading by A-level students who had entered their annual competition. In particular she opined that many students followed an over taught, rigid formula or checklist of features. Moreover, while students tended to do impressive and intricate close analysis they rarely related this to the ideas and effects of poems. In her words, 'many commented on small details without ever trying to come to an overall 'reading' of the poems, or trying to convey anything about what they found special or distinctive about that poet's writing in relation to others'.

Few students, it seems, understand poems as intricately working machines within which each part works in co-ordination with others. Rather than work through a pre-set formula, Ms Bleiman proposed a more open and flexible reading agenda for poetry. As she rightly says, 'if they'd followed through on their instant reactions and trusted them more, they would have been much more likely to get to the heart of what was most interesting about their chosen poems'. The authors would very happily echo these sentiments and,

---

[1] https://www.englishandmedia.co.uk/blog/why-are-students-struggling-to-write-well-about-poetry

we hope, the varied essays in this book demonstrate precisely this sort of responsive and flexible approach recommended by the English & Media Centre. Here is Barbara's 'agenda' for poetry teaching and teaching criticism in full:

Students should:

- Read poetry in a different way from prose, acknowledging what is unique about it as a literary form and enjoying the different kind of reading and critical thinking that this implies
- Have an authentic response to it that is based on what really strikes them – the things that leap out at them as being interesting, unusual or special, trusting their own responses rather than assuming that someone else automatically has a more authoritative view that they need to adopt
- Explore aspects of language and form in relation to the big picture of what the poet is trying to communicate, rather than as micro-analysis for its own sake
- Think about such issues as tone and have the confidence to make a judgment about whether a poem is serious and reflective, wittily playful, or sharply satirical, intensely emotional or highly philosophical
- Subject their interpretations to scrutiny, so that they can justify to themselves [and to others], the grounds for their views and ensure that their readings are plausible and convincing
- Write poetry themselves, to get under the skin of the genre and understand what it means to write in a poetic form or forms. This might include writing their own poetry, writing back to poems,

textual transformations and other experiments with poetry to understand the choices poets have open to them.

- Read adult critical writing about poetry, to develop a sense of the kind of thinking they do and the unique ways in which they engage critically with this particular literary genre.
- Read widely, beyond the confines of examination specifications, to develop confidence, familiarity and pleasure in poetry.

To us that seems like an excellent and wise agenda. And we hope this book provides exactly the sort of incisive critical writing about poetry that will help to stimulate and refine your own individual responses.

Our primary audience for this book is A-level students, but we've included teaching ideas that we hope might be of use to colleagues. [We've used the utterly unoriginal, but universally understood sign of the light bulb to signify a teaching idea. At the back of the book there's also a list of tried and tested revision activities which can be completed individually or with a class.]

AQA Love Poetry Through the Ages and assessment

Obviously we recommend that all teachers and students read the material on the AQA English Literature, specification A website to fully inform themselves about the nuances of assessment. However, what follows is a brief summary of key points and of particularly useful information.

All the exam boards have struggled somewhat with the new 'co-teachable' AS and A-level requirements. AS exams can now be taken as a stand-alone qualification at the end of the lower sixth or, alternatively, students can take an entirely linear A-level course and not be entered for AS levels at all. Some set texts appear both at AS and A-level and some only at one level. AQA A specification's Love Poetry anthology is, however, a set text at both AS and A level. But the assessments of this text vary significantly between AS and A-level.

At AS level students have to answer one question in their exams on one poem from the anthology. This question will ask them to 'examine' a particular critical view on a specific poem which will be printed on the exam paper. AQA has provided the following sample question:

'Examine the view that Elizabeth Jennings presents the married couple in this poem as having entirely lost their love for each other.'

Although there are slight variations on the weightings of each a.o.[2], for all English Literature specifications the assessment objectives are the same:
AO1: Articulate informed, personal and creative responses to literary texts, using associated concepts and terminology, and coherent, accurate written expression. [28%]
AO2: Analyse ways in which meanings are shaped in literary texts. [24%]
AO3: Demonstrate understanding of the significance and influence of the contexts in which literary texts are written and received. [24%]
AO4: Explore connections across literary texts. [12%]
AO5: Explore literary texts informed by different interpretations. [12%]

---

[2] For instance OCR have weightings of 30, 30, 20, 10, 10, putting more emphasis on close analysis and a little less on contexts.

Clearly the first three in this list are the most significant assessment objectives and this is reflected in the specific mark scheme of the poetry exam question. Here the 25 marks available are distributed as follows: AO1: 7, AO2: 6, AO3: 6, AO4: 3, AO5: 3. In short, a strong answer will be well informed, well written, perceptive, analytical and alert to the significance of contexts.

In their mark scheme for poetry AQA give their examiners the following useful prompts to aid marking:

• has the candidate engaged in a relevant debate or constructed a relevant argument?
• has the candidate referred to different parts of the text to support their views?
• has the candidate seen the significance of the text in relation to the central historicist literary concept?
• has the candidate referred to authorial method?
• the candidate's AO1 competence.

AQA's notes on AO3 also provide guidance for teachers and students in terms of narrowing and focusing the potentially huge area of 'contexts':

AO3: In exploring this poem about love, students will address the central issue of how literary representations of love can reflect different social, cultural and historical aspects of the respective different time periods in which they were written.

At A-level students will tackle an unseen task on poetry as well as a comparative essay. Both of these questions will be marked out of 25. The unseen task will feature two poems on the theme of love which students will have to compare. The second poetry question will ask students to compare at least two poems from the anthology with a novel from the list of set texts. The sample question AQA have provided is: 'Compare how the authors of two texts you have studied present barriers to love'.

Rather surprisingly, considering the comparative nature of both these questions, the weighting of the assessment objectives is the same as for the AS exam.

Applying this information to the essays in this book, we have aimed to provide well written and well informed close readings of each poem. Our main focus has been on close analysis of various aspects, such as imagery and form, but often this is informed by significant contexts, literary or historical.

Modern poetry published in Britain

To misquote Andrew Marvell a little, had we but space enough and time we would, of course, provide a comprehensive overview of developments in British poetry from Thomas Hardy through to the most recently published work. Unfortunately, or perhaps, fortunately for you, we have neither the space nor time to produce this here. If you are curious enough to want a comprehensive treatment of developments in poetry in the twentieth century, we strongly recommend *The Oxford English Literary History*, volume 12, Part II, by Randall Stevenson. What will can provide, however, is a whistle-stop tour.

An understanding of literary contexts deepens appreciation of any text. Context may not determine meanings, but it certainly has a significant effect on them. Consider, for instance, the following sentence, 'the duck is ready to eat'. How does the meaning of this sentence change if we change the context? If the context is a restaurant one meaning is clear. But a different meaning is evinced if the context is a pond. Other meanings entirely would come into play if the sentence were heard in a gangster or spy movie. And so on. So, whether they are officially rewarded through assessment objectives or not, contexts [literary, socio-historical and of reception] are always, always significant.

Mainstream and the avant-garde

In all forms of art there is a mainstream and an avant-garde. After T. S. Eliot launched *The Waste Land* on an unsuspecting public in the 1920s and the Modernist Movement swept through the arts world, throwing everything up in the air, a split developed in English poetry that still, arguably, persists to this day. On one side were poets committed to the sort of radical thematic, stylistic and formal experimentalism that Modernism promoted. On the other were poets who considered Modernism to be too radical, excessive and self-obsessed. This second set of poets sought to maintain continuity with earlier, traditional forms of English poetry.

As Peter Howarth writes in *The Cambridge Introduction to Modernist Poetry*, the term Modernism would perhaps better be replaced by Modernisms, such is the diversity of different artistic movements and trends associated with it. Howarth draws a useful parallel with jazz:

'...perhaps the best analogy is to see modernism as an umbrella term: a recognisable genre of music which emerged among various artists who found themselves part of a growing 'movement', rather than being invented singlehandedly at one time or place. Like jazz, it has different but related sub-genres with it [Futurism, Imagism, Objectivism, Surrealism and many others], some intense internal rivalries...and much creative fusion with other art forms.' [3]

However, despite the various sub-genres, we can discern certain trends and approaches common to most Modernist texts. For one thing, as the name implies, Modernist texts wanted to be modern. In the new machine age of the early twentieth century previous modes of art seemed suddenly outdated, redundant, unfit to capture a new reality. A new age needed a new literature, one that was leaner, fitter, more angular, more machine-like, more real. If nothing else, Modernist texts share an antagonism for, and rejection

---

[3] Peter Howarth, *The Cambridge Introduction to Modernist Poetry*, p.4

of, the values and procedures of the Victorian age.

Modernist painters dumped the traditional single perspective; modernist poets binned the metronome of metre and regular form; modernist composers dispensed with melody and regular time signatures and embraced dissonance; modernist architects replaced traditional bricks with steel and glass. Hostility to convention was the vogue. Experimentation ruled. The world reeled before the shock of the new.

The father of modern Psychology, Sigmund Freud, was a pervasive influence: Generally interested in the mind and the workings of the subconscious, Modernist texts tend to explore topics traditionally outlawed as taboo. For example, in novels, Modernists rejected traditional, rational models of character formation, developing instead the 'stream of consciousness' to reveal the subconscious drives supposedly governing characters' behaviour.

Relativist in outlook, Modernists wanted to see the world in a different, less

fixed way. The subject of their art is broken up and broken down. As the image of Juan Gris's 1918 painting, *The Guitar*, illustrates, rather than seeing and presenting their subject from a single, fixed perspective, Modernists favoured presenting multiple, even potentially contradictory, points of view. In the novel, for instance, the Victorian preference for God-like omniscient narration gave way to stories related through the less reliable narration of various major and minor characters. Hence, generally Modernism is characterised by a radical collage approach: Incongruous elements are combined, so that structurally and linguistically texts become assemblies of seemingly disparate fragments. Often drawing on classical literature as a form of ironic intertextual contrast, Modernist works also tend to be self-reflexive - in dialogue with themselves and their own procedures.

Modernism was, and still is, challenging. As anyone who has read *The Waste Land* or tried to read Joyce's seminal Modernist novel, *Ulysses*, will know, Modernist texts tend to be rather taxing on the old grey matter. For its original audience, Igor Stravinsky's modernist masterpiece *The Rites of Spring* was so hard to digest that the first audiences broke out in violent riot. Modernist paintings were frequently considered scandalous and banned.

Consider, as an example, Picasso's famous painting *Les Demoiselles d'Avignon*, painted in 1907, but not first exhibited until 1916, and a prime example of early Modernism in the visual arts: Not exactly a conventional depiction of the female nude is it? Rather than being curvaceous and alluring, the female characters here are angular and rather threatening.

In contrast, traditionalist poets eschewed what they considered to be the self-indulgent excesses, elitism, vogue for fragmentation and the brain-bending difficulties of Modernism. Instead these writers favoured well-crafted, sonorous and coherent poems, poems which aimed to communicate comprehensible meaning to a wide audience. They favoured what might be called the comfort of the old. Focusing on capturing 'the real', antipathetic to anything smacking of redundant Romanticism, illogical mysticism or the foreign fancy avant-gardism of Modernism, these poets championed the traditional craft skills of writing. For them writerly craft and tradition was embodied in the work of the Victorian poet, Thomas Hardy, pictured here.

In his biography of the poet, Ted Hughes, Jonathan Bate usefully outlines developments in twentieth century poetry after Modernism: 'The radical experimentation of T. S. Eliot and Ezra Pound had given way to the political poetry of the 1930's and then in the Forties the passionate rhetoric of Dylan Thomas was a reaction against the cool intellectualism of W. H. Auden. The Movement of the Fifties was, in turn, a reaction against the 'wild loose emotion' of Thomas.' [4]

The Movement poets of the 1950s and 60s gave the traditionalists' emphasis on well-made poems a contemporary, down-to-earth, restrained and peculiarly English spin. These poets often took a detached, ironic role to comment disaffectedly on modern culture and on the experience of the often lone individual within it. Characteristically they combined traditional, regular poetic forms with modern, colloquial English. In doing so they developed a poetic aesthetic that dominated the mainstream of English poetry for many decades. Arguably, indeed, their ideas still have a powerful influence on contemporary poetry. In the AQA anthology Philip Larkin and Elizabeth Jennings are both associated with The Movement.

In the 1960s other strains kicked hard against this mainstream. Notably the work of Ted Hughes and his wife, Sylvia Plath, and, in America, the rhapsodic style of the Beats and the shocking candour of Confessional poets such as Anne Sexton. At the start of the decade, the influential critic Al Alvarez produced an anthology called, tellingly, *The New Poetry* in the introduction to which he argued that poetry had to move beyond the restrictions and  limitations of what he dubbed the Movement's 'gentility principle'. A champion first of Hughes and later too of Plath, Alvarez demanded that poetry be less buttoned-up, more charged with fierce passion, more extreme, more capable, in fact, of expressing the truth of life in an era containing two world wars, concentration camps, and genocide. Poetry had

---

[4] Jonathan Bate, *Ted Hughes, The Unauthorised Life*, pp. 179-180

to up to the task of conveying life in a time haunted by the threat of nuclear obliteration.

Usefully, Plath's poetry embodies a tension between two contrary strains in poetry that are still traceable in the Forward anthology. On the one hand she was influenced by the European symbolist and surrealist poets. Rather than writing directly about their experiences, these poets used the symbolic language of dreams and of myths. Symbolism and the mythic mode can be seen as an attempt to universalise experience, but it also provides some protective cover for a poet. On the other hand, Plath's poetry was shaped by the Confessional style of poetry coming from the States. In contrast to symbolist work, Confessional poets made their own autobiography their chief subject, writing about it in a direct, undisguised style. The courage of Confessional poets lies in the naked exposure of intensely personal details of their often troubled and complex lives. Because of its exploration of taboo subjects, such as extreme emotions, sex, death, addiction, madness and so forth, Confessional poetry was often shocking and controversial. Broadly speaking, the content of Plath's poetry may be nakedly confessional but her treatment applies the veil of the symbolic and surrealist.

Another influential anthology reflecting, but also shaping, the terrain of British poetry was Andrew Motion and Blake Morrison's *Penguin Book of British Writing*, published in 1982. This anthology was notable for its conservative choices [all the poets in Alvarez's anthology were excluded, few female and no black poets were chosen]. In the second half of the twentieth century the radical strain in British poetry continued as a counter to this more commercial mainstream. Its stance and perspective was well articulated by Iain Sinclair in the provocative introduction to his anthology of English poetry, which, even in its title sticks a metaphorical two fingers up to The Movement and its followers. First published in 1996, Sinclair's anthology *Conductors of Chaos* can be seen as a rejoinder to Motion and Morrison. Here's a taste of the introduction:

> The work I value is that which seems most remote, alienated, fractured. I don't claim to 'understand' it but I like having it around. The darker it grows outside the window, the worse the noises from the island, the more closely do I attend to the mass of instant-printed pamphlets that pile up around my desk. The very titles are pure adrenalin: *Satyrs and Mephitic Angels, Tense Fodder, Hellhound Memos, Civic Crime, Alien Skies, Harpmest Intermezzi, A Pocket History of the Soul.* You don't need to read them, just handle them: feel the sticky heat creep up through your fingers....Why should they be easy? Why should they not reflect some measure of the complexity of the climate in which they exist? Why should we not be prepared to make an effort, to break sweat, in hope of high return?

Sinclair goes on to offer some interesting advice on how to read any poem, but especially a radical, avant-garde one:

> There's no key, no Masonic password: take the sequence gently, a line at a time. Treat the page as a block, sound it for submerged sonar effects. Suspend conditioned reflexes...if it comes too sweetly, somebody is trying to sell you something.

Try placing all the set poems in the AQA anthology on a continuum from, at one end, avant-garde/ radical/ experimental and at the other end mainstream/ traditional/ well-made. Repeat the exercise, only this time arrange the poems by their various constituent elements - form, language, themes. Some poems, might, for instance, be radical in terms of content, but more conventional in form, or vice versa. At the end of this process you should develop a sense of which poem is the most radical and which the most traditional in approach. Which is better, or, indeed, whether one style is better than another, is for you to judge.

What might the ultimate radical avant-garde poetry of today look like? Perhaps it might be a poem that seems to reject all the traditional attributes that make a poem a poem. Or dispense with all the traditional tools, such as imagery. More radical perhaps would be a poet that denied themselves the use of anything other than function words. How about a poem made entirely of conjunctions, prepositions and articles? What might that look like? Or more radically still, perhaps, the most avant-garde poets might dispense with words entirely, constructing poems just from punctuation. How would you go about writing, or worse, analysing such a poem? If this seems too far-fetched, spare a thought for the Cambridge English undergraduates who were set a wordless poem constructed just of brackets, question and exclamation marks to analyse in their finals exam [though, to be fair to the university, they were at least given the title]. In this light, reading the Forward anthology poems we've a much easier task.

Tackling the unseen

If Literature is a jungle, of all the beasts that roam or lurk among its foliage, from the enormous, lumbering Victorian state-of-the-nation novel to the carnivorous revenge tragedy, the most dangerous by far is a small, fast-moving beast, a beast untethered by place or time, a beast that is, in fact invisible. This infamous critter is called, simply, 'the unseen'.

Well, that's sounds all rather alarming. Let's bring the rhetoric down a notch or ten. How should you go about analysing an unseen poem and how can you prepare for this demanding task? In this case, by 'unseen' we don't mean the sort of poem those poor undergraduates had to analyse, i.e. a poem without any words, but a poem you see for the first time in the examination hall.

To start with, we need to make clear that we don't believe there's one universally right method for reading poems. If there were, all the varied types of literary theorists - Feminist, Marxist, postcolonial and so forth – would have to adopt the same working methods. Like the children depicted above, critics and theorists do not, in fact, all read in the same way. So, it's vital to appreciate that there's no single master key that will unlock all poems. A uniformly applicable method of reading a poem, or of writing about it in an examination, or for coursework, is like the philosopher's stone; it just does not exist. Or as Iain Sinclair puts it, there's no 'Masonic password' that will give you instant access to the locked inner chamber of a poem's most secret meanings.

Having a singular method also makes the foolish assumption that all poems can be analysed in exactly the same way. A mathematician who thinks all maths problems can be solved with one method probably won't get very far, we expect. Instead you need to be flexible. Trust your own trained reading skills. Respond to the key features of the text that is in front of you as you see them. It's no good thinking you will always write your second paragraph on figurative imagery, for instance, because what are you going to do when confronted with a poem entirely devoid of this feature, such as Ciaran O'Driscoll's Please Hold? Although all the essays in this book explore fundamental aspects of poetry, such as language, form, themes, effects and so forth, we haven't approached these aspects in a rigid, uniform or mechanical way. Rather our essays are shaped by what we found most engaging about each poem. For some poems this may be the use the poet has made of form. This is likely to be the case if, for instance, the poet has used a traditional form, such as a villanelle. For other poems the striking thing might be imagery; for others still it might be the way the poet orchestrates language to bring out its musical properties.

In terms of critical approach, we'd champion well-informed individual freedom above over-regulated and imposed conformity. Hence, we hope our essays will be varied and interesting and a little bit unpredictable, a bit like the poems themselves. We trust that if you write astutely about how a poet's techniques contribute to the exploration of themes and generation of effects, you really won't be going far wrong.

[If you're interested in trying different methods of analysing poems, there is a concise guide in our A-level companion book, *The Art of Writing English Literature essays, for A-level and Beyond*].

To reiterate: Always keep to the fore of your essay the significance and impact of the material you're analysing. Very sophisticated analysis involves exploring how different aspects of the poem work in consort to generate effects. As a painter uses shapes, brush strokes, colours and so forth, or a composer uses chords, notes and time signatures, so a poet has a range of poetic devices at his or her disposal.

Think of a poem as a machine built to remember itself. Your task is to take apart the poem's precision engineering - the various cogs, gears and wheels that make the poem go - and to examine carefully how they operate. If you

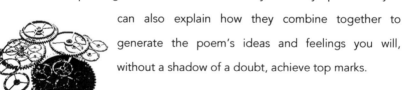

can also explain how they combine together to generate the poem's ideas and feelings you will, without a shadow of a doubt, achieve top marks.

We believe your essays must express your own thoughts and feelings, informed by the discipline of literary study and by discussion with your teachers and peers. And, that your essays should be expressed in your own emerging critical voice. Finding, refining and then trusting your own critical voice is part of the self-discovery that contributes to making English

Literature such a rewarding subject to study at A-level.

Offering quality support material, a safety net, if you like, for your walk on the tightrope of interpretation, we hope the essays offered here will give you the confidence to make it across to the other side. Or to switch metaphors, our essays are designed to provide you with the maps and tools, the essential survival kit in fact, that will help you to thrive in the literary jungle, master this collection of poems and to tame the unseen. In achieving this, you should also achieve great grades in your exams.

Writing comparative essays

The following is adapted from our discussion of this topic in **The Art of Writing English Literature Essays** course companion book, and is a briefer version, tailored to the AQA A-level examination task. Fundamentally comparative essays want you to display not only your ability to intelligently talk about literary texts, but also your ability to make meaningful connections between them. The first starting point is your topic. This must be broad enough to allow substantial thematic overlapping of the texts. However, too little overlap and it will be difficult to connect the texts; too much overlap and your discussion will be lopsided and one-dimensional. In the case of the AQA exam, the board obviously determines the broad topic they want you to discuss, love. The exam question will ask you to focus on the methods used by the poets to explore a particular aspect of this theme. You will also be directed to write specifically on language and imagery as well as other poetic techniques. And, of course, you will also be required to compare poetry to a prose treatment of love.

A three-way comparison can be tricky to handle, so we suggest that in terms of structuring your essay you treat the two poems as equivalent to a single text. You have to choose two companion poems to compare. Selecting the right poems for interesting comparison with the novel is obviously very important. To think about this visually, you don't want Option A, over the page, [as there's not enough overlap] or Option B [two much overlap]. You want Option C. This option allows substantial common links to be built between your chosen texts where discussion arises from both fundamental similarities AND differences. [In the following diagram we've treated the two poems as one text, text A and the prose novel is text B.]

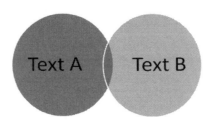

Option A: too many differences

Option B: too many similarities

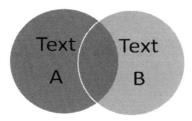

Option C: suitable number of similarities and differences

The final option will generate the most interesting discussion as it will allow substantial similarities to emerge as well as differences. <u>The best comparative essays actually find that what seemed like clear similarities become subtle</u>

differences and vice versa while still managing to find rock solid similarities to build their foundations on.

How should you structure your comparative essay? Consider the following structures. Which one is best and why?

Essay Structure #1

1. Introduction
2. Main body paragraph #1 - Text A
3. Main body paragraph #2 - Text A
4. Main body paragraph #3 - Text B
5. Main body paragraph #4 - Text B
6. Conclusion

Essay Structure #2

1. Introduction
2. Main body paragraph #1 - Text A
3. Main body paragraph #2 - Text A
4. Main body paragraph #3 - Text B
5. Main body paragraph #4 - Text B
6. Comparison of main body paragraphs #1 & #3 - Text A + B
7. Comparison of main body paragraphs #2 & #4 - Text A + B
8. Conclusion

Essay Structure #3

1. Introduction
2. Main body paragraph #1 - Text A + B
3. Main body paragraph #2 - Text A + B

4. Main body paragraph #3 - Text A + B

5. Main body paragraph #4 - Text A+ B

6. Conclusion

We hope you will agree that 3 is the optimum option. Option 1 is the dreaded 'here is everything I know about text A, followed by everything I know by Text B' approach where the examiner has to work out what the connections are between the texts. This will score the lowest AO4 marks. Option 2 is better: There is some attempt to compare the two texts. However, it is a very inefficient way of comparing the two texts. For comparative essay writing the most important thing is to discuss both texts together. This is the most effective and efficient way of achieving your overall aim. Option 3 does this by comparing and contrasting the two texts under common umbrella headings. This naturally encourages comparison. Using comparative discourse markers, such as 'similarly', 'in contrast to', 'conversely' 'likewise' and 'however' also facilitates effective comparison.

When writing about each poem keep the bullet points in mind. Make sure you do not work chronologically through a poem, summarising the content of each stanza. Responses of this sort typically start with 'In the first stanza' and employ discourse markers of time rather than comparison, such as 'after', 'next', 'then' and so forth. Even if your reading is analytical rather than summative, your essay should not work through the poem from the opening to the ending. Instead, make sure you write about the ideas explored in the two poems and the novel, the feelings and effects generated and the techniques the writers utilise to achieve these.

Writing about language

Poems are paintings as well as windows; we look at them as well as through them. As you know, special attention should be paid to language in poetry because of all the literary art forms poetry, in particular, employs language in a precise, self-conscious and distinctive way. Ideally in poetry, every word should count. Analysis of language falls into a number of different categories:

- By diction we mean the vocabulary used in a poem. A poem might be composed from the ordinary language of everyday speech or it might use elaborate, technical or elevated phrasing. Or both. At one time some words and types of words were considered inappropriate for the rarefied field of poetry. The great Irish poet, W. B. Yeats never referred to modern technology in his poetry, there are no cars, or tractors or telephones, because he did not consider such things fitting for poetry. When much later, Philip Larkin used swear words in his otherwise well-mannered verse the effect was deeply shocking. Modern poets have pretty much dispensed with the idea of there being an elevated literary language appropriate for poetry. Hence in the AQA anthology you'll find all sorts of modern, everyday language, including some forthright swearing.
- Grammatically a poem may use complex or simple sentences [the key to which is the conjunctions]; it might employ a wash of adjectives and adverbs, or it may rely extensively on the bare force of nouns and verbs. Picking out and exploring words from specific grammatical classes has the merit of being both incisive and usually illuminating.
- Poets might mix together different types, conventions and registers of language, moving, for example, between formal and informal, spoken

and written, modern and archaic, and so forth. Arranging the diction in the poem in terms of lexico-semantic fields, by register or by etymology, helps reveal underlying patterns of meaning.

- For almost all poems imagery is a crucial aspect of language. Broadly imagery is a synonym for description and can be broken down into two types, sensory and figurative. Sensory imagery means the words and phrases that appeal to our senses, to touch and taste, hearing, smell and sight. Sensory imagery is evocative; it helps to take us into the world of the poem to share the experience being described. Figurative imagery, in particular, is always significant. As we have mentioned, not all poems rely on metaphors and similes; these devices are only part of a poet's box of tricks, but figurative language is always important when it occurs because it compresses multiple meanings into itself. To use a technical term figurative images are polysemic - they contain many meanings. Try writing out the all the meanings contained in a metaphor in a more concise and economical way. Even simple, everyday metaphors compress meaning. If we want to say our teacher is fierce and powerful and that we fear his or her wrath we can more concisely say our teacher is a dragon.

Writing about patterns of sound

 What not to do: Tempting as it may be to spot sonic features of a poem and list these, don't do this. Avoid something along the lines of "The poet uses alliteration here and the rhyme scheme is ABABCDCDEFEFGG." Sometimes, indeed, it may be tempting to set out the poem's whole rhyme scheme like this. Resist the temptation: This sort of identification of features is worth zero marks. Marks in exams are reserved for attempts to link techniques to meanings and to effects.

Probably many of us have been sitting in English lessons listening somewhat sceptically as our English teacher explains the surprisingly specific significance of some seemingly random piece of alliteration in a poem. Something along the lines "The double d sounds here reinforce a sense of invincible strength" or "the harsh repetition of the 't' sounds suggests anger". Through all of our minds at some point may have passed the idea that, in these instances, English teachers appear to be using some sort of Enigma-style secret symbolic decoding machine that reveals how particular patterns of sounds have such particular coded meanings.

And this sort of thing is not all nonsense. Originally deriving from an oral tradition, poems are, of course, written for the ear as much as for the eye, to be heard as much as read. A poem is a soundscape as much as it is a set of meanings. Sounds are, however, difficult to tie to very definite meanings and effects. By way of example, the old BBC Radiophonic workshop, which produced ambient sounds for radio and television programmes, used the same sounds in different contexts, knowing that the audience would perceive them in the appropriate way because of that context. Hence the sound of bacon sizzling, of an audience clapping and of feet walking over gravel were actually recordings of an identical sound. Listeners heard them differently because of the context. So, we may, indeed, be able to spot the repeated 's' sounds in a poem, but whether this creates a hissing sound like a snake or the susurration of the sea will depend on the context within the poem and the ears of the reader. Whether a sound is soft and soothing or harsh and grating is also open to interpretation.

The idea of connecting these sounds to meanings or significance is also a productive one. Your analysis will be most convincing if you use a number of pieces of evidence together. In other words, rather than try to pick out individual examples of sonic effects we recommend you explore the weave or pattern of sounds, the effects these generate and their contribution to feelings and ideas. For example, this might mean examining how alliteration and assonance are used together to achieve a particular mimetic effect. An example will help demonstrate what we mean.

In **Punishment** by Seamus Heaney the speaker 'can feel [...] the wind / on' the dead woman's 'naked front' and the description of how the wind 'shakes the frail rigging / of her ribs' emphasises delicacy. Heaney also uses gentle alliteration of soft r-sounds together with the brittle short i-sounds in 'rigging' and 'ribs' to reinforce this fragility. This crafting of soundscapes is reflective of a wider strategy in the beginning stages of the poem. The first two stanzas are full of subtle sound patterns where a proliferation of soft n-, l- and s-sounds are subtly snagged on harsher fricatives and plosives. The n-sounds of 'ca<u>n</u>', '<u>n</u>ape', '<u>n</u>eck', 'wi<u>n</u>d', '<u>n</u>aked', 'fro<u>n</u>t', '<u>n</u>ipples' are counteracted by the k-sounds in 'ne<u>ck</u>', 'na<u>k</u>ed' and 'sha<u>k</u>e' in particular. This conflict in sound connects to the wider issues of individual conflict with collective expectations in the poem.

Writing about form & structure

As you know, there are no marks for simply identifying textual features. This holds true for language, sounds and also for form. Consider instead the relationship between a poem's form and its content and effects. Form is not merely decorative or ornamental: A poem's meanings and effects are generated through the interplay of form and content. Broadly speaking the form can either work with or against a poem's content. Conventionally a sonnet, for instance, is about love, whereas a limerick is a comic form. A

 serious love poem in the form of a limerick would be unusual, as would a sonnet about an old man with a beard.

Sometimes poetic form can create an ironic backdrop to highlight an aspect of content. An example would be a formally elegant poem about something monstrous. The artist Grayson Perry uses form in this ironic way. Rather than depicting the sort of picturesque, idealised images we expect of ceramics, Perry's pots and urns depict modern life in bright, vivid colours. The urn pictured, for instance, is entitled Modern Family and depicts two gay men with a boy who they have presumably adopted. A thrash metal concert inside a church, a philosophical essay via text message, a fine crystal goblet filled with cherryade would be further examples of an ironic relationships between message and medium, content and context or form.

****

Put a poem before your eyes. Start off taking a panoramic perspective: Think of the forest, not the trees. Perhaps mist over your eyes a bit. Don't even read the words, just look at the poem on the page, like at a painting. Is the poem slight, thin, fat, long, short? What is the relation of whiteness to blackness? Why might the poet have chosen this shape? Does it look regular or irregular?

A poem about a long winding river will probably look rather different from one about a small pebble, or should do. Unless form is being employed ironically. Think, for instance, about how Michael Symmons Roberts uses form in *To John Donne* to convey tentative and contemplative thought. Now read the poem a couple of times. First time, fast as you can, second time more slowly and carefully. How does the visual layout of the poem relate to what it seems to be about? Does this form support, or create a tension against, the content? Is the form one you can recognise, like a sonnet, or is it, perhaps, free verse? Usually the latter is obvious from irregularity of the stanzas and line lengths.

As Hurley and O'Neill explain in *Poetic Form: An Introduction*, like genre, form sets expectations: 'In choosing form, poets bring into play associations and expectations which they may then satisfy, modify or subvert'. [5] We've already suggested that if we see a poem is a sonnet or a limerick this recognition will set up expectations about the nature of the poem's content. The same thing works on a smaller level; once we have noticed that a poem's first stanza is a quatrain, we expect it to continue in this neat, orderly fashion. If the quatrain's rhyme scheme is xaxa, xbxb, in which only the second and fourth lines rhyme, we reasonably expect that the next stanza will be xcxc.

[5] Hurley & O'Neill, *Poetic Form, An Introduction*, p.3

So, if it isn't we need to consider why.

So after taking in the big picture in terms of choice of form now zoom in: Explore the stanza form, lineation, punctuation, the enjambment and caesura. Single line stanzas draw attention to themselves. If they are end-stopped they can suggest isolation, separation. Couplets imply twoness. Stanzas of three lines are called tercets and feature in villanelles and terza rima. On the page, both these forms tend to look rather delicate, especially if separated from each other by the silence of white space. Often balanced through rhyme, quatrains look a bit more robust and sturdy. Cinquains are swollen quatrains in which the last line often seems to throw the stanza out of balance.

Focus in on specific examples and on points of transition. For instance, if a poem has four regular quatrains followed by a couplet examine the effect of this change. If we've been ticking along nicely in iambic metre and suddenly trip on a trochee, examine why. Consider regularity. Closed forms of poems, such as sonnets, are highly regular with set rhyme schemes, metre and number of lines. The opposite form is called 'open', the most extreme version of which is free verse. In free verse poems the poet dispenses with any set metre, rhyme scheme or recognisable traditional form. What stops this sort of poetry from being prose chopped up to look like verse? The care of the design on the page. Hence we need to focus here on lineation. Enjambment runs over lines and makes connections, caesura pauses a line and separates words. Lots of enjambment generates a sense of the language running away from the speaker. Lots of caesuras generate a halting, hesitant, choppy movement to lines. Opposites, these devices work in tandem and where they fall is always significant in a good poem.

Nice to metre...
A brief guide to metre and rhythm in poetry

Why express yourself in poetry? Why read words dressed up and expressed as a poem? What can you get from poetry that you can't from prose? There are many compelling answers to these questions. Here, though, we're going to concentrate on one aspect of the unique appeal of poetry – the structure of sound in poetry. Whatever our stage of education, we are all already sophisticated at detecting and using structured sound. Try reading the  following sentences without any variation whatsoever in how each sound is emphasised, and they will quickly lose what essential human characteristics they have. The sentences will sound robotic. So, in a sense, we won't be teaching anything new here. It's just that in poetry the structure of sound is carefully unusually crafted and created. It becomes a key part of what a poem is.

We will introduce a few new key technical terms along the way, but the ideas are straightforward. Individual sounds [syllables] are either stressed [emphasised, sounding louder and longer] or unstressed. As well as clustering into words and sentences for meaning, these sounds [syllables] cluster into rhythmic groups or feet, producing the poem's metre, which is the characteristic way its rhythm works.

In some poems the rhythm is very regular and may even have a name, such as iambic pentameter. At the other extreme a poem may have no discernible regularity at all. As we have said, this is called free verse. It is vital to remember that the sound in a good poem is structured so that it combines effectively with the meanings.

For example, take a look at these two lines from Marvell's *To his Coy Mistress*:

'But at my back I alwaies hear
Times winged Chariot hurrying near:'

Forgetting the rhythms for a moment, Marvell is basically saying at this point 'Life is short, Time flies, and it's after us'. Now concentrate on the rhythm of his words.

- In the first line every other syllable is stressed: 'at', 'back', 'al', 'hear'.
- Each syllable before these is unstressed 'But', 'my', 'I', 'aies'.
- This is a regular beat or rhythm which we could write
  ti TUM / ti TUM / ti TUM / ti TUM , with the / separating the feet.
  ['Feet' is the technical term for metrical units of sound]
- This type of two beat metrical pattern is called iambic, and because there are four feet in the line, it is tetrameter. So this line is in 'iambic tetrameter'. [Tetra is Greek for four]
- Notice that 'my' and 'I' being unstressed diminishes the speaker, and we are already prepared for what is at his 'back', what he can 'hear' to be bigger than him, since these sounds are stressed.

- On the next line, the iambic rhythm is immediately broken off, since the next line hits us with two consecutive stressed syllables straight off: 'Times' 'wing'. Because a pattern had been established, when it suddenly changes the reader feels it, the words feel crammed together more urgently, the beats of the rhythm are closer, some little parcels of time have gone missing.

A physical rhythmic sensation is created of time slipping away, running out. This subtle sensation is enhanced by the stress-unstress-unstress pattern of words that follow, 'chariot hurrying' [TUM-ti-ti, TUM-ti-ti]. So the hurrying sounds underscore the meaning of the words.

14 ways of looking at a poem

Though conceived as pre-reading exercises, most of these tasks work just as well for revision.

1. <u>Crunch it [1]</u> – This means re-ordering all of the text in the poem under grammatical headings of nouns, verbs, prepositions and so forth. If this is done before reading the poem for the first time, the students' task is [a] to try to create a poem from this material and [b] to work out what they can about the style and themes of the original poem from these dislocated grammatical aspects. An alternative is to list the words alphabetically and do same exercise. Re-arranging the poem in grammatical categories after reading can also be a useful analytical task.

2. <u>Crunch it [2]</u> – This is another exercise that can be used as an introductory activity before reading a poem for the first time or as a useful revision task. Rearrange the poem into groupings based on lexico-semantic fields. Show students one group of words at a time, asking them to write down what the each group of words might tell us about the poem's themes & style. Alternatively, split the class into small groups and give each one group of words. Ask them to suggest possible titles for the poem.

3. <u>Crunch it [3]</u> – In this method students have to reduce each line of the poem to one key word. If they do this individually, then in pairs, then as a class, it can facilitate illuminating whole class discussion and bring

out different readings. We've applied the cruncher at the end of each of the following essays.

4. <u>Cloze it</u> [aka blankety-blank] – A cloze exercise helps students to focus on specific choices of vocabulary. Blank out a few important words in the first couple of stanzas and as much as you dare of the rest of the poem. Make this task harder as the course goes on. Or use it for revision to see how well the poem's been remembered.

5. <u>Shuffle it</u> – Give students all the lines in the poem but in the wrong order. Their task is to find the right order. Make this a physical exercise; even older pupils like sticking cut up pieces of paper together! Start off with reasonably easy activities. Then make them fiendishly hard.

6. <u>Split it</u> – Before a first reading, post a few key lines from the poem around the classroom, like clues for literary detectives. Arrange the class into small groups. Each group analyses only a few lines. Feedback to the class what they have found out, what they can determine about the poem. Ask them how the information from other groups confirms/ changes their thoughts. Finish by getting them to sequence the lines.

7. <u>Transform it</u> – Turn the poem into something else, a storyboard for a film version, a piece of music or drama, a still image, a collage of images a piece of performance art. Engage your and their creativity.

8. Switch it – Swap any reference to gender in the poem and the gender of the poet. Change every verb or noun or metaphor or smile in the poem. Compare with the non-doctored version; what's revealed?

9. Pastiche or parody it – Ask students to write a poem in the style of one of the poems from the anthology. Take printed copies in. Add your own and one other poem. See if the students can recognise the published poem from the imitations. A points system can add to the fun.

10. Match it [1] – Ask students to find an analogue for the poem. Encourage them to think metaphorically. If they think Burnside's History is like a thrash metal song by the The Frenzied Parsnips they'll really need to explain how.

11. Match it [2] – Take some critical material on about 5 or 6 poets; there's good stuff on the Poetry by Heart and Poetry Archive websites. Take one poem by each of these poets and a photo. Mix this material up on one page of A3. The students' task is to match the poet to the critical material and to the image. To add to the creative fun you could make up a poem, poet and critical comments.

12. Complete it - Give the students the first few lines of the poem. Their task is to complete it. If they get stuck and plead profusely and if you're feeling especially generous you can give them a few clues, such as the rhyme scheme or the stanza form.

13. Write back to . If the poem's a dramatic monologue, change the point of view and write the other character's version of events. What might be the silent thoughts of the woman in *Talking in Bed*? What might the Sexton's lover have to say if he could reply to her poem?

14. Listen to it - Tell the class you're going to read the poem once. Their task is to listen carefully and then write down as much of it as they can remember, working first on their own and then in pairs. Read the poem a second time and repeat the exercise. Discuss what they did and didn't remember.

I have a dark and dreadful secret. I write poetry.

Stephen Fry

Edna St Vincent Millay, *I, being born a woman and distressed* [Sonnet XLI]

This poem is one that is proudly feminist from the get-go. The narrative voice makes itself heard from the very beginning, declaring an identity defined by gender: 'I, being born a woman'. This is a bold statement, with its impact reinforced by the fact that the first word of the poem is placed on a strong beat. This effect is further heightened by the use of punctuation, with the comma creating a deliberate pause that accentuates the prominence of the first person pronoun and emphasising its independence. This first line truly sets the tone for the rest of the poem and encapsulates its overarching theme, which is the narrative and sexual agency of an independent female voice. This is a poem that is unapologetic about its strident tone and daring attitude towards sexual freedom. It explores the idea of sex as something separate from marriage or indeed love. Published in 1923, just as the 'Roaring Twenties' were getting under way and America and most of Europe were beginning to enjoy unprecedented levels of social, economic, and cultural activity, having largely recovered from the horrors of the First World

War, the poem's frank attitude towards female sexuality and empowerment was unusually outspoken, even for its time.

Subversion

The choice of form for this poem is telling; it is a sonnet, the most traditional of vehicles used by poets to explore and express the idea of love. To be more precise, Millay chooses to shape her writing into the technically demanding form of a Petrarchan sonnet, which follows the rhyme scheme a b b a a b b a c d c d c d, and manages this form with considerable panache. Petrarch was an Italian poet who lived during the time of the Renaissance, in the 14th century. Although he did not invent this particular formal structure, it is his works which popularised the form and which were most widely translated, appreciated and emulated by writers working in the English language during the 16th century. One of the most famous sonneteers in the history of English literature is, of course, Shakespeare, whose sequence of 154 poems explored the themes of love, mortality, and beauty. Millay's poem is thus formally very traditional, as it closely follows the expected rhythms and rhymes that have been used throughout literary history by [mostly male] writers, extolling the virtues of their significant others. It is thus significant that Millay has chosen such a proudly female voice as her narrator; it is as if she has laid claim to the form, made it her own territory and wrenched it free from the predominantly male grasp of literary history.

Millay is keenly aware of the way in which her depiction of feminine identity differs from traditional stereotypes, and she plays on this in the very first lines of the poem:

'I, being born a woman and distressed

By all the needs and notions of my kind'

The first line, when taken on its own, can be seen to represent a more traditionally derogatory depiction of women as weak and easily upset; this effect is achieved though the adjective 'distressed'. However Millay uses enjambment to carry the first line through to the second, quickly revealing a self-awareness regarding this generalisation with its reference to the playfully alliterative 'needs and notions' of her gender. The second line of the poem quickly overturns any potential negativity to be found in the first line and subverts the reader's expectations.

One of the most refreshing things about this poem is its sense of humour. The description of the narrator as being left 'undone' by their sexual encounter can be interpreted as a cheeky pun. This adjective could simply refer to the fact that she has deviated from her intended course of action, in the sense of 'alas! I am undone', but it could also be a reference to her state of undress, with buttons having become unfastened. Additionally, in the final section of the poem, when narrator declares that she will not 'season / My scorn with pity', but instead 'make it plain', a cooking metaphor is used to flavour the poem's message. Women have traditionally been depicted as belonging 'in the kitchen', responsible for domestic chores and expected to inconvenience themselves to please and support their male partners; this is a stereotype that continues to rear its ugly head even today. However, by stating that she will  only be 'plain' in her mode of communication, the narrator appears to reject this role of the woman as homemaker. Unwilling to alter her words to soothe any bruised egos, she also refuses to play a conventionally lady-like or gently feminine role. Indeed, she even goes as far as to refuse conversation altogether. Millay's cooking metaphor also links to the idea of the sexual appetite as a hunger that must be satisfied.

Another way in which the poem subverts traditional expectations is in its strong emphasis in the poem upon the physical aspect of sex. This is partly demonstrated in the way in which the 'you' of the poem is not initially referred to directly in the poem. Instead, the poem's addressee is positioned in terms of their physical self and its relationship to the narrator: 'your propinquity', 'your person', 'your body'. This has the effect of emphasising the distinctly carnal, physical nature of the relationship between the narrator and the person they are addressing. The person being addressed by the narrator is thus effectively objectified, denied any real agency or active role. It is implied that they are male, although their gender is never explicitly stated. Here Millay reverses the more familiar pattern in traditional sonnets of women being the silent and passive objects of men's admiration. The Petrarchan blazon, for instance, is a convention in which parts of a woman's body are anatomised and celebrated. Millay's tone is cooler, less celebratory, less physical than her male forebears. Her poem makes no mention of 'love' at any point; indeed, it appears to reject emotions altogether, instead focusing on the narrator's struggle between physical impulses and rational restraint.

Clarified pulse vs. clouded mind
The physical and the intellectual are set up in direct opposition to one another throughout the poem. This effect is achieved through the use of antithetical pairs, linked together with alliteration; we first have '**cl**arify the pulse and **cl**oud the mind', and, later, 'my **st**out blood against my **st**aggering

brain'. However, it is important to note that these opposing forces are all internal to the female narrator; the person to whom the poem is addressed is not shown to play an active role in this conflict and indeed is depicted as being almost irrelevant. Although the narrator describes herself as being left 'undone, possessed' by their sexual encounter, the effect seems to be more of a spiritual 'possession', or madness, rather than a physical sense of ownership. Through the use of this particular noun, Millay perhaps refers back to the time when women were considered to be the property of their husbands; this was the case in England until as late as 1882, when the

The Final "No!"

"Whar? Give up my freedom to become your slave? Not in a thousand years!"

Married Women's Property Act finally recognised wives' independent legal identities. As such, the fact that the narrator describes herself as 'possessed' by her own sexual impulses, rather than by her partner, can be seen as a reaction against the history of women's subjugation to men. Indeed, marriage, like love, is notably absent from Millay's poem. Developments in contraception over the 19th and early 20th centuries meant that women were increasingly able to engage in sex for its own sake, without the need to worry about marriage or children. The sexual emancipation boasted about by Millay's narrator was undoubtedly to some extent influenced by this medical development.

Petrarchan sonnets are traditionally structured in two halves: the first eight lines, the octave, sets out an initial problem or idea, while the final six lines, the sestet, develops this in some way and achieves a resolution. In a traditional Petrarchan sonnet, the octave is further separated into two groups of four lines, or quatrains. However, in Millay's poem, the strength of the narrator's sexual drive, and its ability to override her rationality, is reflected in the way in which the word 'zest' breaks through the traditional separation between the fourth and fifth lines, blurring the boundaries between the first and second quatrains. Overall, however, Millay adheres quite strictly to the form that she has chosen; there are no half-rhymes, or any particularly unconventional rhythms in the metre that she uses. The contrast between the tight control that the poet demonstrates over her use of language and the poem's exploration of an individual woman's lack of sexual inhibition thus encapsulates the depicted conflict between the intellectual and the physical.

We could read the poet's formal discipline as an attempt to rationalise and control the sexual impulses that she describes. This attempt at control can also be seen in the way in which Millay's depiction of physical attraction uses rather distancing, scientific terms. For example, the word 'propinquity' is complex, abstract and somewhat formal word, while Millay uses anatomical terms to describe her sexual urges: 'pulse' and 'blood' compete against her

 'brain'. This picking apart of the narrator's physical body by naming its separate elements also reflects the poet's sense of internal division and self-contradiction. The choice of narrative perspective also contributes to the sense of conflict; the poem is in first person and refers to 'you' throughout, and so the reader could be placed both in the position of the narrator as well as seeing themselves as being addressed directly.

Strength and vulnerability

Although 'fume of life' may bring to mind perhaps the pheromones, or subtle smells, that are used by animals to communicate with one another, and which scientists have shown to play a role in sexual attraction between humans, this scientific concept was only discovered in the 1950s, decades after the composition of this poem. 'Fume of life' is instead perhaps a reference to a line from Shakespeare's play *Romeo and Juliet*, where the titular hero claims that:

> 'Love is a smoke raised with the fume of sighs;
> Being purged, a fire sparkling in lovers' eyes;
> Being vexed, a sea nourished with loving tears.
> What is it else? A madness most discreet,
> A choking gall, and a preserving sweet.'

This little speech depicts love as being a contradictory influence, both bitter and sweet. However, Millay replaces 'sighs' with 'life'; for her, the physical act of sex is held separate from any emotional implications and is perhaps instead driven by basic human biology. Interestingly, its portrayal in the poem seems also to be devoid of pleasure. Perhaps echoing Shakespeare's description of love as a kind of 'madness', Millay describes sex as an act of 'frenzy'. Interestingly, the line 'to **b**ear your **b**ody's weight upon my **b**reast' with its heavily plodding alliterative consonants does not seem to celebrate the physical enjoyment of sex, but instead depicts it as a burden, or indeed even an inevitability that has not been desired.

Perhaps hidden within the strong approach taken by Millay is a sense of vulnerability. For example, the narrator describes herself as having been 'born a woman', rather than simply just declaring that she *is* a woman. This

implies that the narrator has been acted upon and that she has had no choice in the matter, thus creating a sense almost of helplessness. The narrator is depicted as almost the victim

of her own impulses, which are held separate from her, she is 'left...undone' by her desires and is actually, surprisingly, not given an active role to play in the poem. Although it is true that she is attracted to the person she addresses, finding their person 'fair', she is 'urged' to this by their proximity. If we examine the verbs used throughout the poem, we find that they are actually somewhat passive: 'distressed', 'urged', 'feel', 'leave', 'think', 'remember', 'find'. This effect is reinforced elsewhere in the poem in the way in which we see her physical urges ['blood' and 'pulse'] overwhelming her intellect ['mind' and 'brain']. The narrator does not wield her sexual urges, but is rather used by them. This sense almost of self-betrayal is reflected in her use of the phrase 'poor treason'. Additionally, there is a feeling of inevitability to the sexual activity described by the narrator; the one depicted in the poem is described as having happened 'once again', and the line 'when we meet again' implies that this situation will repeat itself.

To conclude then, this poem is proudly unashamed of female sexual desire and provides an unusually candid perspective on its role in an individual's psychology. In this poem, sexual urges are depicted in biological and anatomical terms, and placed in opposition to reason and intellect. We are shown the narrator's relative indifference to the person she is addressing, and her cold dissection of the mental and physical processes that lead her to sexual encounters. Hence Millay refuses to present herself in conventional gender terms as a weak, gentle or emotional woman. Cleverly appropriating the sonnet, the traditional vehicle used by male poets to explore the theme of love, Millay uses it instead to depict the complete absence of love from the act of sex. Yet, despite the poem's undeniably powerful female voice, there remains an undercurrent of vulnerability, and of perhaps a sense of the self as a victim of its own powerful urges.

'Crunching' a poem means reducing each line to its single most important word. Obviously which word is most important is open to critical debate. Have a go yourself at crunching all these poems and then compare with our choices.

I, Being crunched

WOMAN – KIND – URGED – ZEST – BEAR – FUME – CLOUD – POSSESSED – TREASON – BRAIN – LOVE – PLAIN – FRENZY - AGAIN

Robert Frost, *Love & a Question*

The question that makes up the title of Robert Frost's **Love and a Question** is not "Evening, mate. Fancy a threesome with a well-travelled stranger wielding a symbolic phallus?" Well, hopefully not. Frost's poem ignites various uncomfortable questions about loves plural and love of the plural itself. In essence there is a question, never voiced directly in the poem, about

choosing between selfish and selfless love. The moral quandary of the poem sees a man presented with a simple choice: [a] shelter a poor misfortunate stranger and display a rare love of his fellow man OR [b] get rid of him as quickly as decorum allows and indulge in the love of his new wife's body. While it could be argued that both scenarios provide pleasure for another, option [b] does entail a

significant amount of self-gratification into the bargain. Yet again, human weakness wins out and selfishness and sexiness reigns supreme. But the choice is not guilt-free and there is a certain haunting quality at the poem's end.

I think we're alone now

The poem opens with the type of setting utilised by many a recent horror film: a Stranger [note the capitalisation] calls to the door of a house in the middle of nowhere at night. Now while such films claim to be based on true events [i.e. there are lots of isolated residences in the world] not many would bother to capitalise the potential pest intruding on our loved-up couple. It is a strange decision and must bestow some form of importance on the stranger that 'came to the door at eve'. The mini-narrative that Frost dramatises in the poem is as spare as the leafless woodbine trees of the setting, which surely encourages us to view the "Stranger" as potentially symbolic as well as real. If this is the case, what does he symbolise? The newlyweds stand on the threshold of a new life and maybe this Stranger relates to the new strangeness of being man and wife. The gender of the Stranger ['He'] suggests the 'bridegroom fair' if this is the case. The fact that the Stranger is denied shelter by the married couple could imaginably signal bad omens for the new marriage; the end of the poem certainly suggests this in its 'harbouring of woe in the bridal house'. If the Stranger is the future bridegroom then the refuge that marriage should provide is going to be as protective as the leafless woodbine trees.

Even if we jettison all notions of latent symbolism, if we see the Stranger as real, he certainly presents an oddness that echoes the wider oddness of the situation. The most striking sense of oddness is in the 'green-white stick in his hand'. Now, it wouldn't be unusual for a drifter to carry a stick, but Frost puts such emphasis on its colouration that it deserves careful deciphering. Green is most obviously associated with nature, but also safety [green traffic lights] and healing while white has obvious connotations of innocence and purity; it can also represent successful beginnings. The facts that this Stranger also carries the 'burden' of 'care' to the bridal door implies that how he is treated will have profound consequences for the 'bridegroom fair'. The Stranger's dislocated status is also reflected in the lack of open communication between the pair and this intensifies the mystery of the situation: 'he asked with the eyes more than the lips'. This gesture seems almost like an invitation in itself, an invitation to interpret the situation correctly. Interestingly, the speaker is not the one who asks but the one who answers. And the more the 'bridegroom' talks the less impressive he begins. Those who know most say least and all that!

Lose-lose situation: stupid or selfish, or both?

The bridegroom's decision making is revealed as leaving a lot to be desired. The Stranger's viewing of 'the road afar / without a window light' shows a route devoid of comfort and guidance. It makes it pretty clear to the reader that the decent thing to do is to provide the shelter required by the kindly traveller. Note the clever soft alliteration of the w-sounds that bestows poignancy on even having to consider such a hard journey. The bridegroom's assertion that 'I wish I knew' is borderline moronic given the careful presentation of the world around the two men. The poetic speaker informs us that the 'woodbine leaves littered the yard' and how 'the woodbine berries were blue'. The first image suggests complete lack of shelter and feelings of exposure or vulnerability, while the blue berries symbolically imply the coldness of the night in question. Just in case we missed it the speaker tells us that 'winter was in the wind'. Alliteration again makes this detail stand out and also gives a lovely soft sadness to the phrase that snags our sympathy. It is only after these obvious details that Frost allows our bridegroom to wish he knew – it may be safe to assume his bride didn't marry him for his intelligence or at least his generosity of spirit.

Which is when the poem switches from bridegroom to bride. It's a brief cameo role but an important one as her 'face rose-red with the glowing coal' provides a significant contrast of inside warmth and outside cold. Again, the reader is lead to contrast the two in a way that magnifies everything they have that the poor kindly stranger does not – again the decision should be obvious. However, the bride's face is not just heated from without; it is also heated from within. 'The thought of the heart's desire' together with the

'rose-red' flushing [and the symbolic 'fire' of the previous line] reveal her patient anticipation of the sexual pleasure. Symbolically, of course, red is associated with passion and sex [and possibly danger] but the soft alliteration of the r-sounds and the hyphenated coupling of 'rose' with 'red' endows it with a romance that seems natural, a naturalness that complicates the choice between sexual gratification and brotherly love. It isn't as easy as one demonised option versus a saintly alternative. This section of the poem is heavy with broad, pondering assonance, especially the long o-sounds i.e. 'over the open'; 'rose-red with the glowing coal'; 'thought' 'bridegroom looked at the weary road'. The effect is to slow the pace down, almost mimicking the bridegroom's gazing at his wife – it is long, slow and sensual. Hence why he 'looked at the weary road / yet saw but her within'. Maybe this new development allows us to understand his previous indecisiveness. If it does, then he eschews generosity and charity for selfish sexual pleasure, which won't endear him to our hearts. What also may affect his ability to endear himself will be how the reader interprets the last two lines of the third stanza. Onn first impressions it seems to articulate the bridegroom's optimistic hopes for the future and sees an eloquent elevation of his bride by storing her 'heart in a case of gold [...] with a silver pin'. However, the imagery of precious metals suggests the purity of his new wife's love, but it is significant that it is not her heart but the 'case' which is 'gold'. In other words it is the display container that seems more important than what is contained within. Feminist readers will surely baulk at the phallic penetration of the female heart 'as it is pinned with a silver pin' where the repetition of 'pin' magnifies the penetrative violence enacted. Phallic penetration is also sonically enacted with a flurry of sharp, narrow i-sounds in the assonance of 'within / and wished her heart in a case of gold / and pinned with a silver pin.' Again, it is the 'pin' rather than the 'heart' that is endowed with precious metal. Even if one refuses to indulge a reading that laments patriarchal oppression of the female in all its gory penetrative phallic glory, it cannot be denied that the symbolism of gold and silver commodifies their love in some way.

Mixed-up love aka 'The Bad Lovers' Guide'

With this ornamental elevation seared onto the reader's mind, Frost brings us back to the moral dilemma. It is solved rapidly. The bridegroom leaves the thinking to the trousers department and 'thought it little,' which is a subtle way of telling us that passion rather than charity wins out. The bridegroom fobs the Stranger off with 'a dole of bread, a purse, / [and] a heartfelt prayer'. Note Frost's use of the adjective 'dole' which suggests the bare minimum so as not to be insulting. The 'heartfelt prayer' is surely ironic given the fact that he doesn't have to pray to God to help 'the poor' – all he has to do is open up his home to a caring Stranger. Similarly, the 'heartfelt [...] curse' 'for the rich' seems disingenuous, as in effect he curses himself, a man who 'thought it little to give / [...] a purse,' a man clearly much richer [remember the silver and gold imagery] that the vulnerable traveller. So long kind Stranger!

However, while the physical exit of the Stranger is actioned quickly [and notably without any explicit description at all] the poem ends in murky ambiguity 'The bridegroom wished he knew'. However, what he is uncertain of is also uncertain. <u>What does Frost mean when he states the bridegroom did not know 'whether or not a man was asked / to mar the love of two / by harbouring woe in the bridal house'?</u> It should be quite simple: he either was asked or he wasn't. <u>So why can't he be sure?</u> If he wasn't asked the Stranger must have seen the situation and gone on his freezing way. Frost's phrasing does not help matters if

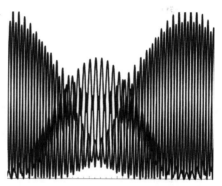

we look closely at 'To mar the love of two / by harbouring woe in the bridal house'. What two does this refer to? The most obvious interpretation is that the love of husband and wife is marred by bringing the Stranger into their home. But what if the 'two' refers to both his wife and the Stranger? <u>Does this mean that the bridegroom is in a no-win situation, that no matter what he does regarding this decision it will end with the 'harbouring [of] woe in the bridal house' because one type of love must trump the other?</u> Maybe it's a simple as a guilty conscience after rejecting the Stranger; maybe he does not know how his guilt will feel as he makes love to his wife. Maybe he worries that guilt may impact upon his husbandly duties. The verb 'harbouring' suggests a hiding of such woe, which may indicate that it is hidden by the bridegroom and only time will tell how much his conscience pricks him after the event or how much woe it will bring.

Forks in the road

The uncertainty of decision-making [check out Frost's *The Road Not Taken* or *Stopping by Woods on a Snowy Evening*] and the process of returning to reflect upon the consequences of decision making is embodied in Frost's chosen form. His octaves present indecision in their indented lines [as if they can't make up their mind where to place themselves] and suggest a visual self-division as each line oscillates between one starting place and another. A similar indecision presents itself in the varying line lengths which alternate between 4-beat line and 3-beat lines. The majority of 4-beat lines contain 9 syllables [instantly an odd number for metrical analysis]. Frost's metre is predominantly iambic, but there is a notable elasticity in the metre with an extra unstressed syllable usually floating around each line. Such hypermetrical constructions and their unpredictable placement also add an element of uncertain movement to the poem. It could even be seen to reflect the moral weakness of the bridegroom who cannot make the morally superior choice. Additionally the rhyme scheme of ABCBDEFD presents a clear sequential sonic journey [ABC] only to jump back to [B] before going onto a new set of sounds with a similar retrograde effect.

The final stanza is notable for its alternation between loose iambic tetrameter lines and perfectly iambic trimeter lines, for example:

'The bride groom thought it little to give

A dole of bread a curse'

This sonic construction mimics the vacillation from certainty to uncertainty, from conviction to doubt. Importantly, while the poem ends with perfect iambic trimester, the uncertainty of the expression as well as the loss of syllables suggests something important has been lost in this decision: The bride groom wished he knew. Love, in some, way has been damaged but which love [of the individual [his wife] or the collective [the Stranger]] remains to be seen.

Crunch and a Question

STRANGER – BRIDEGROOM – GREEN-WHITE – CARE – ASKED – SHELTER – ROAD – WITHOUT – PORCH – LOOK – QUESTION – STRANGER – LITTERED – BLUE – WINTER – WISH – BRIDE – FIRE – GLOWING – DESIRE – WEARY – HER – CASE – PINNED – LITTLE – DOLE – HEARTFELT – CURSE – WHETHER – MAR – WOE – WISHED

Charlotte Mew, *A Quoi Bon Dire*

Same difference

'What's in a name? That which we call a rose / By any other name may smell as sweet', so says Shakespeare's Juliet. However, the title of a poem is often carefully chosen by the poet, and it can change the meaning of the rest of a work - see, for example, September 11th, 2001 by David Herd. The title of a poem is the first thing that the reader encounters, and it creates a sense of expectation, setting the scene for the words that follow. A quoi bon dire translates from French as 'What's the good of speaking'. This is a daring move - the poem has barely begun, and Mew already seems to question its own value as a means of communication.

By giving a French title to her poem written in English, Mew makes a statement regarding the way in which the same thing can be said in many different ways, by different people, and using different words. And it is the poem insists the same thing. The poem expresses an apparent paradox; viz. that though the feeling of being in love may feel private, special and unique to particular lovers it is at the same time a universal experience, experienced here both by the narrator as well as by the representative 'boy and girl'. And no matter the means of delivery, these feelings remain the same. <u>Does this weaken the value of individual human expression and experience, if each experience or expression of love is never truly unique?</u>

A theme of separation runs through the poem - separation between the narrator and their beloved, as well as between the couple and the rest of society. But there is a deeper, special connection between the former, one that perhaps even goes beyond death and between these them and the 'boy and girl'. This is a poem that appears ambivalent about love, and about the role played by language in expressing it. However, the poem could also be read as seeking to validate and, indeed, celebrate a form of illicit, transgressive love. But we'll come on to that later.

Me, you and everybody else

The poem begins with two stanzas that explore a past relationship experienced by the narrator. Here, the  relationship between the poet and their significant other, the 'you' of the poem, is contrasted against 'everybody' and their apparent lack of understanding. What everybody 'thinks' and 'sees' is shown to be inaccurate, as public perception cannot comprehend the ostensibly unique, deeply personal, private relationship between the narrator and significant other. The couple are portrayed as having the ability to perceive that which is beyond surface appearance, with their relationship existing despite what appears to be a seventeen year separation, and the resultant effects of time. Mew depicts this relationship between the narrator and the person that they are addressing as being situated outside of society, as well as almost outside time itself. If we take the word 'dead' literally, their relationship even survives mortality. The first stanza opens with two sibilant lines that seem to audibly reinforce the sense of privacy and seclusion that the poet creates around this relationship:

'Seventeen years ago you said
Something that sounded like Good-bye'

Repeated 's' sounds create a softened, almost whispering effect. This sense of intimacy is further reinforced by the way in which the poem is addressed directly to the reader, in the second person - we are drawn into this private relationship with the narrator, and cannot help but participate in the narrative as it unfolds. Paired adjectives and pronouns, such as 'stiff and cold', 'this and that' and 'boy and girl', highlight the emotional pairing throughout the poem of 'I' and 'you', as well as the contrasting pairing of the couple, who are set against the uncomprehending and unsympathetic 'everybody'.

The separation of the couple from those around them and from each other is shown by the way in which the lines 'But I' and 'But you' are much shorter metrically than the preceding lines sharing the same stanza, and really stand out from the rest of the poem, drawing the reader's attention. 'I' and 'you' are both cut off from the rest of the poem, and also from each other; this sense of separation is further underlined by the use of emphatic full stops between stanzas. The appearance of these short lines on the page is abrupt, with the curtailment of the stanza reflecting also perhaps the way in which romantic relationships can isolate couples from others around them. For this couple, focused entirely on their significant other, the world has shrunk; the rest of society is indistinct and excluded. This process can generate negative as well as positive feelings. The repetition of the first person pronoun between the first and second stanzas: 'But I. / So I, as I', for instance, suggests isolation and potential loneliness. The insistence of this repetition when combined with the use of halting punctuation creates a feeling almost of desperation, hinting perhaps at the limitation of the first person narrative mode as a kind of entrapment within a single perspective. This questioning of the narrative voice returns us to the poem's title, 'what's the good in speaking'. The poem's ambivalent attitude towards language itself is reflected in its use of the first person narrative mode, which seems to indicate that all speech is necessarily limited by one's individual point of view. The masculine rhyme scheme also contributes to the sense of enclosure and isolation.

The last stanza breaks free from the tight structural precedent set by the first two stanzas, with five lines instead of four; these lines are also metrically stretched in contrast to the poem's initially disciplined rhythmic pattern. This reflects the poem's opening up to introduce new ideas, looking beyond the relationship between the narrator and their beloved to add a new dimension and force a change of perspective. The 'you' and 'I' of the poem are no longer isolated in this final stanza; they share the stage and are contrasted with 'some boy and girl'. Where the majority of the other lines in the poem are in iambic tetrameter, Mew stretches the second line in this stanza, 'some boy and girl will meet and kiss and swear', adding one extra beat on at the end. This extension is emphasised by the poet through the repetition of the simple conjunction 'and' - there are three in this line alone, and the resulting long-voweled assonance contributes to the sense of growth and expansion. In this way, the poem's structure reflects the way in which its scope has been expanded, looking beyond the initially limited world of the narrator and their lover that was created in the first two stanzas. This effect is further heightened by the fact that all the words in this line are monosyllabic; this creates a plodding, almost monotonous rhythm, perhaps also emphasizing that these actions are not unique and that other couples repeat the same gestures to express their love. This is also hinted at earlier in the poem, where the lover says 'something that sounded like Good-bye'; the exact details of what was said may be irrelevant - it is the sentiment that remains the same and is shared by others elsewhere and everywhere, despite any couples' beliefs to the contrary.

The relationship between the boy and girl of the final stanza is contrasted with that of the narrator and their lover, which was carefully set out in the first two stanzas. 'Their' love is shown to be equivalent or at least comparable to that which is shared by the narrator and their lover, who are located 'there' - the link is made through the use of homonyms, words that have identical spelling or pronunciation, but which have different meanings. The use of these words creates an audible doubling that connects the two couples. Love is clearly depicted as being a universal human experience; despite each individual couple's fervent beliefs to the contrary, that 'nobody can love their way again', these declarations are repeated by others, elsewhere in the world, throughout time. The idea that these feelings extend beyond the individual and can be generalised is reflected in the grammatical choices made by the poet. For example, in the line 'one fine morning in a sunny lane', the determiners 'one' and 'a' are both general, rather than specific. The avoidance of a definite setting gives the stanza and indeed the poem as a whole a sense of wider applicability, as well as of timelessness. This is also reinforced in the use of modal verbs in the final line of the poem, which features the future perfect tense: 'will have' and 'shall have' seem to combine both the future and the present. The use of the second person pronoun 'you' throughout the poem contributes to its sense of timelessness and general applicability, as the narrator's voice speaks not only to their lover but also to an undefined public.

Universal and private stories

Returning to the line 'and one fine morning in a sunny lane', we can see that it also seems to echo the typical fairy tale opening, 'once upon a time'. By recalling one of the stock phrases used to preface folk and fairy tales, Mew returns us once more to the idea of all human experiences as having been lived or narrated before by others. After all, folk and fairy tales epitomise the idea of narrative as following a series of set templates. Everybody knows to expect the same tropes, themes, and patterns of action: the hero, the damsel in distress, the fairy godmother, the happily ever after. These types of narratives also tend to address universal human issues such as family relationships, love, and using one's strengths to overcome adversity. Mew is very selective with the number of adjectives that she uses, and the final stanza's 'fine' and 'sunny' contrast with the 'stiff and cold', 'old', and 'dead' of the first two stanzas. Overall, the final stanza seems to be more optimistic in its approach towards love. The fact that love and its rituals are shared by others throughout time and space is not necessarily a negative thing. The fact that the final stanza is looser and more fluid in its structure could also reflect the fact that the recognition of the connectedness of human experiences across individual relationships can be a type of liberation. Although the relationship between the narrator and their partner exists in the past, the recognition that the same emotional experiences are repeated elsewhere provides a sort of hope and continuation. The relationship from seventeen years ago is, in a way, carried on in the present as well as into the future by other couples.

A quoi bon dire was published in Mew's first, critically acclaimed collection of poetry, The Farmer's Bride, in 1916. By this point Mew had already been making a living from some journalism and other writing, but it was this collection that really cemented her place in literary society of the time. Mew's family was beset by trouble; one of seven children, three of her brothers had died, and two more siblings committed to mental hospitals by the time she was in her twenties. Mew and her remaining sister struggled financially after the death of their father in 1898, and also vowed never to marry, to avoid continuing the history of mental illness in their family. Mew is widely thought to have been a lesbian, although there is no evidence that she had a sexual relationship with any women. <u>Does this biographical information change your view of the poem and its portrayal of relationships, separation, and the link between the personal and the universal?</u>

Perhaps for instance we can flip round our previous interpretation: Rather than the boy and girl's love being shown to be equivalent or at least comparable to that which is shared by the narrator and their lover, it is the narrator's relationship that is shown to be the equivalent or at least comparable to the boy and girl's. Going back to our suggestion that the poem could be about forbidden, transgressive love if we read the addressee of Mew's poem as being a female lover, then the poem would normalise their illicit, lesbian relationship by equating it to ordinary, socially acceptable heterosexual love.

If we accept this interpretation why didn't Mew make her point more explicitly? Good question. Perhaps the point is that this specific love is the same as the universal experience of love. Perhaps too the poem is guarded, or coded, about a subject that would have been considered taboo to discuss openly in Mew's world. Perhaps the fact 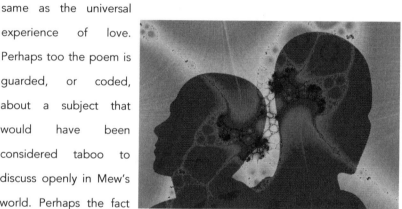 that the poem might have a secret meaning for the specific intended lover, as well as a more general meaning for a more general reader, creates another level or layer of intimacy, a private thrill that links the 'you' and 'I' and excludes the 'them'. Composed of seemingly straightforward, ordinary and literal language, this poem might be expected to have a transparent meaning. But the apparent simplicity is misleading a form, perhaps even of misdirection.

Biographical interpretations of works of art can, however, be risky. It can be too easy to assume emotions and thoughts that were perhaps never there.

Roland Barthes, in his 1967 essay *The Death of the Author*, argued that interpretations of literature that are based on aspects of an author's identity can be too limited in their approach.

And there are no indications throughout the poem of any sort of specific setting or time; it is a work that is difficult to date without any background knowledge of the poet. The 'you' of the poem is never given any specific identity, not even a gender or an age. Indeed, we cannot even be certain that their relationship with the narrator is a romantic, let alone lesbian, one. It is possible to argue that the poem is addressed to a family member or friend, rather than a lover. Regardless of the exact nature of the relationship, however, the themes of love, loss, and the intensity of shared experiences remain applicable. 'What is the point of speaking', says Mew - is it significant that she has not phrased this as a question? Although framing the title of her poem as a statement could imply a sense of resigned pessimism, the poem itself seems largely positive about the value of human relationships and acts of expression. The poem is also teasingly coy in the way in which it sets out the relationship between the narrator and the audience; we are seemingly granted an intimate insight into the private world of the narrator and their intimate, special relationship with their significant other, but are also denied any real information through deliberate indeterminacy and a lack of specific detail.

A *quoi* crunched:

SEVENTEEN – GOODBYE – DEAD – I – COLD – GOODBYE – EVERYBODY – YOU – SUNNY – SOME – NOBODY – WHILE – SMILED

Elizabeth Jennings, *One Flesh*

What happens to couples whose relationship is like the one Philip Larkin depicts in *Talking in Bed*? They might decide to cut their losses and call it a day; they might make a superhuman effort to put right whatever's wrong in their relationship and end up much happier as a result. Or they might end up like the couple Elizabeth Jennings describes in **One Flesh** – a poem whose opening words, 'Lying apart', echo Larkin's 'Lying together'. [Jennings and Larkin knew each other at Oxford; her obituary in the Daily Telegraph notes that they used to listen to jazz records together and they are often bracketed together as Movement poets]. In this poem, Jennings describes an elderly couple whose marriage has settled over the years into a state of silent coexistence, the passion of early married life washed away by time. It's only at the end of the poem that Jennings reveals, devastatingly, that the people she describes are actually her own parents.

Not unity, but distance

The poem takes its title from a verse in Chapter Two of the Book of Genesis. We are told of the creation of Adam, from a handful of dust, and then of Eve, from one of Adam's ribs. The union of Adam with Eve – who Adam describes as 'bone from my bone, and flesh from my flesh' – is established as the model for marriage, in which 'a man leaves his father and mother and is united to his wife, and they become one flesh'. Yet right from the start of the poem, what marks out the couple in *One Flesh* is not unity, but distance. They are 'Lying apart now, each in a separate bed', and are engaged in their own different pursuits. Initially, this could appear peaceful and restful: 'He with a book, keeping the light on late, / She like a girl dreaming of childhood'. However, there's an underlying awkwardness there. His book is unread, while she is only 'like a girl' – she is actually staring at the ceiling, 'her eyes fixed on the shadows overhead'. They lie as if awaiting 'some new event', but it's not clear at this point what this might be. [By the end of the poem, we suspect that this 'new event' might actually be death – the final experience this couple must confront].

The poem's second stanza builds on this sense of uneasiness. A telling simile captures how the couple are 'tossed up like flotsam from a former passion' – like the wreckage of a ship, floating on the sea of life. Yet this is clearly not a stormy relationship. Look at 'how cool they lie'. There's a multitude of meanings packed into this simple seeming line, all of them carefully balanced against each other: 'Cool' can mean casual, or lacking heat – and this lack of heat can itself be comfortable, refreshing, or chilling and indifferent. And 'lie', of course, can refer to their physical position – or to a lack of truth. Their separateness is reiterated, very simply, in the words 'They hardly ever touch', but then this is qualified by a very telling afterthought: 'Or if they do, it is like a confession / Of having little feeling – or too much'. Whatever it is that the couple still feel for each other – love, affection, resentment, frustration, indifference – they certainly do not know how to express it. Instead, what faces them is 'chastity' – a lack of physical intimacy, an absence of sex, and the 'destination / For which their whole lives were a preparation'. It's a pretty bleak prospect.

The Poetry Archive website praises Jennings' work for its 'emotional restraint' and 'unassuming technical craft'. The former is certainly in evidence in *One Flesh*, but it's interesting to see how much it depends on the latter. The first stanza consists of one long sentence, but it's a sentence that begins with a build-up of adjectival and noun phrases that we must make our way through before we get to the main active verb, 'is', in the second half of the fourth line. And even when we get to this main verb, it's immediately postmodified by 'as if'. The overall effect is of stasis – the couple are frozen, as if in a photograph. In turn this creates unease as we anticipate some sort of development – mirroring, of course, the couple lying in their separate beds as if awaiting 'some new event'. There are long, mournful vowel sounds in 'late', 'light', 'like' and 'wait', a predominance of soft consonants such as 'l' and 'w' and 's', and an ABABAA rhyming pattern in the first two stanzas in which the first and third lines are half-rhymes – establishing, very quickly, a sense of quiet dissatisfaction. In the second stanza, the rhyming words in the A lines – 'passion', 'confession', 'destination' and 'preparation' are what's known as feminine rhymes, words where the stresses fall on the penultimate syllable, leaving the rhyming syllables unstressed. It's a fitting technique to use in a poem about a relationship that hasn't been blown apart, but has simply slid into complacency. Notably the B rhymes are, of course, all masculine. Neatly on a structural level this rhyme scheme first separates As and Bs and then brings them together in a couplet at the end of each stanza, suggesting a deeper connection between the two characters than their surface separation implied.

In the final stanza, the rhyming pattern changes to ABABAB, a subtle shift that gives a sense of reaching some kind of development and perhaps resolution. It begins with a line that sums up this couple's relationship, united by time and habit but seemingly not much else: they are 'strangely apart, yet strangely close together'. The silence between them is described in a simile – 'like a thread to hold / And not wind in' – which suggests that they are aware of the distance between them but unwilling [or unable?] to do anything to break it. The metaphor that follows this – 'And time itself's a feather, /Touching them gently' – underscores the sense of a relationship that is being gradually eroded by the passing of the years, in a way that's barely noticed. The delicate images Jennings uses – holding a thread, being touched by a feather – could be seen as a sign that there is still some tenderness left in this marriage. For whatever reason, however, the couple is unable to access it.

The poem ends with a question, and it's only in this final sentence that the narrator reveals that the couple are her mother and father. The passion that once existed between them – the 'fire from which I came' – has died down, 'grown cold', and they have become old almost without noticing the passing of the years. There's a sense that Jennings [who was 40 when this poem was published] is questioning not only whether her parents recognise what has happened to their marriage, but also what this means for her, looking at them from the vantage point of her own adulthood. But the poem doesn't push this train of thought any further: instead, it leaves it as a possibility, in its characteristically observant but unobtrusive manner.

Not distance, but unity?

Of course, there's another possible interpretation, supported by the rhyme scheme and some of Jennings' choices of phrase: Perhaps the couple are so close that they don't need to demonstrate this closeness – they are happy to give each other 'their own space', to sink into companionable silences. See, for instance, how the mirroring phrase 'strangely apart, yet strangely close' both separates and links them. Or consider how many times Jennings uses the plural pronouns, 'they', 'their' and 'them'. The couple is seen entirely through the eyes of Jennings-as-narrator, and this gives her a power to depict their relationship in whatever way she chooses, presenting them through her own particular filter. Maybe she has misinterpreted the feelings her parents had for each other; maybe, given a right of reply, they'd tell a very different story. But all of this is outside the text, and the words on the page are all we have to go on – words that quietly but firmly point out the ironies in the poem's title.

One Flesh crunched:

APART – LATE – DREAMING – WAIT – NEW – SHADOWS – FLOTSAM – COOL – CONFESSION – FEELING – CHASTITY – WHOLE – STRANGELY – SILENCE – TIME – GENTLY – TWO – COLD

Louis MacNeice, *Meeting Point*

She's all states, and all princes, I

Unlike many of the other poems in this post-1900 selection, such as Heaney's interrogation of the artist's response to atrocity or Millay's cool dissection of her own motivations or Larkin's glum musings, MacNeice's poem is properly romantic. With his sharp journalistic technique the poet quickly establishes both a contemporary scene in a coffee shop, with physical table and chairs and a tangible couple, and at the same time a timeless one in which two lovers are suspended and isolated from the world's cares in a self-contained, mutual bubble of love. An interesting co-text for this poem would be John Donne's *The Sun Rising* which also features two lovers escaped from the world and from time.

A photograph and a film

Key to the success of the whole thing, of course, is the description and evocation of the spell of suspended animation. The poem introduces a number of variations of essentially the same image, of stasis:

- The stopped escalator
- The lovers 'neither up nor down'
- The bell 'silent in the air'
- The waiter who does not come
- The clock that has 'forgot them'

Some images, and lines, are recycled, most obviously at the end of each stanza, but also through the body of the poem as a whole - 'time was away and somewhere else' and 'the bell was silent in the air'. Bells are used to signal starts and ends, and this bell is held in suspension both at the start and at the end of the poem. Hence we develop the sense that we keep coming back to where we started, as if time has stopped. Or we're caught in a sort of time loop. Each stanza, in cinquain form, also follows the same pattern - five lines with the same rhyme scheme, adding to the sense of going around the same loop. Moreover Time operates rather oddly in the poem; within the freeze frame bubble some things are in motion, such as the stream, the camels, the distant radio and the woman's fingers. Hence Time is simultaneously stopped and moving. The static couple are simultaneously in a photograph and a film.

Not only has Time been displaced, so have the lovers and space itself. For instance, either they are simultaneously in the coffee shop and near a stream flowing through heather, or the stream is somehow cocooned within the coffee shop. When the poet says 'the desert was their own' where are we, still in the coffee shop or now in the desert? It seems the latter huge space is enfolded in the former infinitely smaller one. And, as in dreams, solid material reality becomes unfixed and fluid too; things inexplicably transform from one thing to another. Firstly, held mid-swing, a bell becomes a flower. That's not a hard transformation to imagine – bell and flower share the same basic shape. However, being both 'brazen' and at the same time making 'no noise', the image suspends apparent or near opposites. Upping the ante, a little later is the desert image, of 'space between cup and plate' which distorts and stretches to incorporate 'miles of sand'. Sound warps too; the dance on the radio synaesthetically transforms, becoming 'like water from a

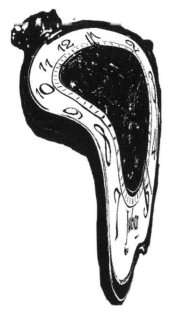

rock'. Turning the surrealism dial all the way up to near max., flicked fag ash reassembles itself, and morphs into 'tropic trees'. Dust, like ash, is, of course, dead. This dead ash blooming again is therefore a condensed image of resurrection, the ultimate cheating of Time. Achieved just by the casual flicking of fag ash. And instantly, magically, as if in extreme fast-forward these trees spread to form 'forests'. As in a Salvador Dali painting, while some of these objects go naturally together, others are incongruous. We have the tables, chairs, waiter, radio and a room which all fit nicely into a realistic coffee shop scene. But we also have displaced and irreconcilable items, such as a bell, an escalator, a British country scene [streams and heather], a desert, camels, a starry night sky and then suddenly forests of tropical trees.

Indeed, there is something rather Dali-esque about MacNeice's poem, but the poet's surrealism is gentler and more subtle than the celebrated

painters'; we feel more grounded in the familiar, solid reality of the coffee shop with its cups and two lovers. Reality may be bending and operating according to new [love] rules, but it is also anchored by the image of two couples in a shop.

The poem's unusual metre adds its contribution to the feeling of distorted, stretched and suspended time. It kicks off at skipping pace. The opening refrain line, 'Time was away and somewhere else' could either be scanned as a trochee followed by three iambic feet: STRESS – unstress, unstress – STRESS, unstress – STRESS, unstress – STRESS, or as a dactyl followed by trochees. In either case the first few beats set a high, hurrying pace, aided by the dynamic swishing sonic qualities of 'was away'. Within the first four beats of the poem Time has already exited speedily from the scene. Scan the rest of the stanzas and you'll discover they keep to an irregular four beat tetrameter which is a song metre. Strong rhymes and repetition of lines and syntax add to the poem's overall songlike qualities.

<u>What is the effect on the lovers of being in love?</u> Reality-changing, obviously as MacNeice says explicitly in the final stanza, 'And life no longer what it was'. Serenaded by the music of the stream and radio, the lovers also feel empowered and protected by their love. They describe the 'desert' proprietorially as 'their own' and they 'had forests'. They're carefree too, immune to disasters in the outside world, 'not caring if the markets crash'. Like Gods they control fate, making plans to 'portion out the stars and dates' and, as we have already noted, God-like, they create instantly multiplying new life, casually without effort, through flicking away some fag ash.

For the majority of the poem the couple are also described through one pronoun, 'they'. Of course, this accords with the idea established in the opening that though they sit on two chairs and drink from two cups, they are connected at a deeper, emotional level, sharing 'one pulse'. The desert is 'their' own, the waiter forgets 'them'. Only towards the end of the poem is the woman referred to separately when 'her' fingers flick away the ash. She, it seems, is the source of new creation. The delayed use of the pronoun 'she', held back until the last stanza, adds poignancy with the tenderly simple phrase 'and she was here', the single source of this magic, light and warmth ['glow'] - all that really matters. The poem is riddled with language and imagery of uncertainty. Time and space are elastic, things are displaced, condensed, distorted in a dream-like fashion. Reality is vague and liminal: Time is away and 'somewhere else'; 'somebody' stopped the escalator, things are 'neither' one thing 'nor' another - they are 'between', 'although', 'whatever'. Even God is uncertain and vague; it is 'God or **whatever** means the good' who / which should be praised. But at the end of the poem all this uncertainty is dispelled. The experience is 'understood' and the heart can 'verify' the experience. And it is the beloved who brings this enlightenment.

Notice how the poet modestly effaces himself from the poem; there's not even a single mention of what he does. This adds significance to the female character and to the poem's poignancy. The factual sounding title, *Meeting Point*, also signals things coming together, him and her becoming 'they'. What would happen if the pronouns were switched so that 'they' became 'we', 'their' → 'our', 'them' → 'us', 'she' and 'her' → 'you'? Why not present the poem in this way to a class and see what difference it makes to their reading of it?

Perhaps by choosing a third person perspective MacNeice avoids the poem becoming too slushy and sentimental. The use of 'we' might make the lovers seem rather precious in their love cocoon. The choice of an omniscient perspective also adds to the sense of the lovers inside their own bubble, sealed off, secure. We, the readers, are watching them from the outside, offered a window into their world. But also, because the thoughts and feelings expressed are clearly those of the poet [such as 'God or whatever means the good / be praised'] this perspective allows him to be simultaneously inside as well as outside the experience. In the last line, for instance, he refers to the woman not being 'there' but 'here', where he is. Another example of the poem's out-of-body / out-of-time displacement that adds to the sense of love's capacity to transport us into the extraordinary.

The *Meeting Point* crunch:

TIME – TWO – ONE – STOPPED – ELSE – NEITHER – FLOWING – ALTHOUGH – NOT – SILENT – HOLDING – BTWEEN – CALYX – BELL – CAMELS – STRETCHED – DESERT – PORTION – MILES – AWAY – FORGOT – WIATER – SOMEWHERE – ASH – BLOOMED – CRASH – FORESTS – HER – GOD – PRAISED – HEART – VERIFY – GOOD – SHE – LIFE – BELL – GLOW – TIME

Anne Sexton, *For my Lover*

'You can't write this way. It's too personal'

'The confessional poetry of the mid-twentieth century dealt with subject matter that previously had not been openly discussed in American poetry. Private experiences with and feelings about death, trauma, depression and relationships were addressed in this type of poetry, often in an autobiographical manner. Sexton in particular was interested in the psychological aspect of poetry, having started writing at the suggestion of her therapist.' [6]

Certainly that's one way of reading Sexton's poem **For my Lover, Returning to his Wife**. The title, for one thing, suggests confessional poetry. Contemporary readers were sometimes shocked by the candour of confessional poems, and Sexton's title could be viewed as vulgar, brazen and even shameless. She has engaged in extra-marital affair, her partner has committed adultery and rather than being ashamed or hiding this fact she

---

[6] https://www.poets.org/poetsorg/text/brief-guide-confessional-poetry

makes it the title of her poem, waving it like a flag. This parading of one's dirty washing in public would have been shocking to many readers in the 1960s, when the poem was first written, and for some readers it's probably still shocking or perhaps just distasteful today. Notably the rest of the poem is addressed to the lover who we imagine as a silent partner in the scene Sexton composes. The title, however, betrays the fact that the poem is also something of a performance piece too, flaunting itself provocatively to the public as well as to the lover.

In addition to the let-it-all-hang-out subject matter, we might point also to the poem's strong sense of a voice in conversation, a colloquial voice at that: 'she is all there', 'favourite aggies', 'let's face it', 'if you glance up'. Add to this the repeated, emphatic use of the egocentric 'I' pronoun and the use of taboo language ['for the bitch in her'] and there's a fair case for reading the poem as a stark version of what one critic pejoratively called Sexton's 'outspoken soap-opera' style.

There's a feminist angle to the poem too. Sexton presents herself and her anger frankly; she doesn't conform at all to the conventional housewife figure of 1960s America: She is not demure or sexually pure; she does not accept a subordinate role; she's not going to shut up, especially when she's got venomous things to say. In fact it sounds as if she wore the trousers in the relationship – 'I give you back heart / I give you permission'. And those judgemental, admonitory adjectives could be flipped

round and worn as war medals in the battle of the sexes: shameless →
unapologetic; shocking → truthful; brazen → brave; vulgar → uninhibited.
Reading the poem in this autobiographical way makes the sort of simple
equation between author and narrator so warned against in literary criticism.
And it's a bit of critical dead end. Either you condemn Sexton for breaking
taboos or you respect and admire her. What's much more striking about the
poem actually is its extraordinary vivid imagery.

'Littleneck clams out of season'

The poem's imagery develops an antithesis, contrasting the female narrator
character with the other female, the wife. But it is a lopsided comparison; far
more of the imagery concerns the wife than the narrator, who seems more
concerned with her rival than she is with the virtually invisible male character.
Initially the love rival is described in a way that suggests she is the perfect
model wife, 'melted carefully down' for her husband and 'cast up';
dehumanised, she is malleable marriage material. We are not told who has
done this melting, but the care with which it is done, suggests the wife may
has been hand-picked as a suitable match. She is also, improbably, 'all
harmony' which suggests a sweet wifely nature. Other imagery signals,
however, that this character is not merely a sort of living doll wife. The wife is
also not entirely associated with domesticity; she 'sees to oars' of the
marriage 'dinghy', a metaphor that suggest movement and potentially
adventure. She can be exciting and dangerous, like 'fireworks' and though
manufactured she is real, not synthetic, like a 'cast-iron pot'. We talk about
'cast-iron' guarantees, things you can utterly rely upon and this image implies
solidity. It's not a flattering description, though, is it, particularly if we think in
terms of physique. It's hard to imagine any woman welcoming being
compared to a pot. Ditto for being compared to a 'monument'.

For much of the poem it seems, at least on the surface, that the narrator rather admires the wife. She describes her rival as 'exquisite', as romantic [setting 'wild flowers at the window'], as having produced beautiful children ['three cherubs drawn by Michelangelo'], as maternal and indefatigable. The description seem generous, rising above jealously, to acknowledge the other woman's qualities, even how they surpass the narrator's own: 'She is all there' and 'she has always been there' compares favourably to 'I have been momentary' and there is the direct comparison in the other woman's favour of 'she is more than that'.

Hence it comes as a shock when the tone changes seventh stanza. Now the wife is presented as dangerous, angry, hurt and potentially vengeful. She has a 'fuse' inside her like a bomb, and a 'flare under her ribs'. There's something crazy and unpredictable about her too; the 'throbbing' inside her, 'the drunken sailor' in her 'pulse'. It's noticeable that the earlier descriptions concerned actions and outside appearances

whereas these final ones focus on the seething anger lying under the surface. But even here there is sympathy perhaps too, such as the visceral image of the wife's hurt and how she has had to hide it; 'the burying of her small red wound alive'.

The wife may dominate the poem, but the narrator also presents herself vividly. In part the description is through implication; outlining the qualities of the wife encourages the reader to infer those of the narrator. So, saying that the wife is 'all there' implies that the narrator is not. Sexton also uses a series of striking metaphors. The narrator is definitely unpot-like: she's like a 'luxury' item, a special, delicious treat such as 'clams out of season'; she's exotic, bold and attractive, like a 'bright red sloop' [who'd choose to ride in the marriage 'dinghy' if the sloop was available?]; she's like a painting - she is 'a watercolour', but one that can be washed off. She's 'momentary', an 'experiment'. And she's dangerous too with her hair 'rising like smoke'. There's no smoke without fire, they say. But the most vivid way in which the narrator is depicted is through the distinctive voice Sexton evokes.

Volatile elements

It's a strong, almost strident, energetic voice that speaks in bold declaratives. It's marked by emphatic repetition. Look for instance at the first two stanzas and how four out of six of them start with 'She is/was or has' and in which the word 'cast' appears three times. Or towards the end of the poem how five lines in succession begin with 'for the...' to build rhetorical momentum. And here the word 'call', used to describe the hold the wife has over her husband, is used four times in five lines. It's a powerful voice too, as we have previously noted, taking command of the situation and the relationship, 'I give you permission' and shifting into the imperative, 'climb her'. An alarming, unsettling voice too. The tone at times is hard to establish. How should we read the seemingly tender phrase 'my darling', the only such phrase that appears in the poem? Or how are we to hear the word 'exquisite' particularly in the light of the 'pot' image that follows soon afterwards? Is it sarcastic? Are some of the apparently more positive images barbed, back-handers? Is the tone arch, or does it veer erratically? Listen to Sexton reading her poem and you'll still not be sure. And it's not just the tone that seems erratic and unpredictable. Lines and images jump illogically from one thing to another: The wife is 'fireworks' is one moment and a 'pot' the next - hard images to reconcile; the narrator tells us she is a 'luxury', offering us the image of the 'sloop' and unseasonal 'clams' by way of example. But how does the image of her rising like smoke fit? How does that suggest luxury? Non-sequiturs are common, such as 'This is not an experiment. She is all harmony'. The speed with which we shift between very different images – sloop / smoke/ clam also contributes to the poem's surreal, uneven quality.

Of course the unpredictability is writ largest in the free verse form of the poem itself. Although the majority of stanzas are quatrains, two are longer and the final one shorter. Line length is more highly variable, with some lines abruptly truncated, such as the opening one, just four short syllables long and others ten syllables or more. The shortest sentences are just three words, 'she is solid' and 'I wash off', whereas the longest, opening with 'I give you permission' stretches over thirteen lines. In this sentence, suddenly, two thirds of the way through the poem, hyphens are used extensively. Ever since Ezra Pound articulated the aesthetics of Imagism, some poets have rejected metre as a mechanical constraint on expression. Iambic pentameter, in particular, was seen by some writers as old rope that had had the life well and truly flogged out of it. Sexton dispenses with metre entirely, so there is no governing pattern of beats underpinning her lines. And there's no rhyme pattern either to keep things in shape. The overall effect is of the stanza form only just about holding the poem's volatile elements together.

The overall impression of the narrator may be of an unpredictable and potentially erratic character. But it is also a speaker capable of beautiful and tender expression, such as the image of children, 'like delicate balloons resting on the ceiling'. Whether this speaker is or isn't Sexton is something of a moot point.

We mentioned that *For my Lover* was written in the 1960s and in many ways the poem embodies the counter cultural elements that would lead to the epithet 'swinging' being attached to this decade. There's the throwing off of inhibitions - rejecting conventional and conservative social mores in the blatant and unashamed treatment of an extra-marital affair. There's also the feminist aspect of a woman speaking frankly and forcefully, rejecting contemporary models of subordinate domestic feminity. And the form of the poem is also rebellious, dispensing with key poetic conventions such as closed and regular form, metre and set rhyme schemes. In some senses too this is an American aspect of Sexton's writing – free verse was embraced much more enthusiastically in the land of the free than back in England, where at a similar time to Sexton our next poet, Philip Larkin was writing. Two poets with more different approaches, attitudes and styles than Sexton and Larkin it is hard to imagine.

For my crunched Lover:

SHE – MELTED – CAST – FAVORITE – ALWAYS – EXQUISITE – FIREWORKS – REAL – MOMENTARY – SLOOP – SMOKE – CLAMS – MORE – GROWTH – EXPERIMENT – OARS – BREAKFAST – SAT – CHILDREN – CHERUBS – OUT – GLANCE – BALLOONS – CARRIED – SUPPER – PERSON – SLEEP – I – PERMISSION – FUSE – BITCH – WOUND – ALIVE – FLARE – DRUNKEN – MOTHER'S – CALL – CURIOUS – BURROW – RIBBON – ANSWER – SINGULAR – SUM – MONUMENT – SOLID – ME – WASH

Philip Larkin, *Wild Oats*

What does the phrase 'sowing your wild oats' mean? It's an expression that conjures up images of youthful excess, a carefree recklessness about sexual relationships before settling down to the responsibilities of marriage and parenthood. It's therefore an ironic title for Philip Larkin's poem about his relationship with Ruth Bowman, the schoolgirl he met whilst working as a librarian in Wellington, Shropshire, in 1943 – a relationship that, so far as the poem goes, seems to have been neither reckless nor particularly pleasurable. [In later life, Bowman remembered Larkin as being 'relaxed and cheerful, entertaining and considerate', a description of him that is particularly unexpected considering the poet's Eeyorish reputation]. Taken as a whole, this is a poem about disappointment and disillusionment, about a relationship that seems from the start to have been marked by Larkin's sense of his own inadequacy.

Life stories

As **Wild Oats** is an autobiographical poem, let's sketch in a few facts. When Larkin and Bowman met, he was 21 and she was 16. According to James Booth, who has written widely on Larkin, Bowman was 'a real, serious-minded schoolgirl' who was 'dazzled' by Larkin, the Oxford graduate and aspiring poet who had ended up in her small Shropshire town in his first job after leaving university. They read poetry to each other and Bowman stole a copy of Yeats' poems from her school library to give to Larkin. In May 1948, they became engaged. Their relationship ended in September 1950, when Bowman wrote to Larkin to break off their engagement, just as he was moving to Belfast to take up a new post as sub-librarian at The Queen's University. [By this time – and unbeknown to Bowman – Larkin had already embarked on the long-term relationship with Monica Jones, lecturer in English at Leicester University, that was to last until his death in December 1985]. Shortly after he first met Bowman, Larkin described her in a letter to his friend Jim Sutton as 'the only girl I have met who doesn't instantly frighten me away'. Yet in Wild Oats, there's none of this warmth and companionship. Instead, Bowman is presented as a compromise, the less attractive of the two girls – a prime example of the gap 'between what Larkin expects of love and what it provides' that has been identified by Andrew Motion as one of Larkin's most persistently-explored topics.

The narrator's colloquial, confiding voice is established right from the first line of Wild Oats, with the casual 'About twenty years ago' [the poem was written in 1962, so the events described in the poem actually took place nineteen years previously]. The poem records Larkin's first meeting with Bowman, when she was accompanied by her friend Jane Exall. Significantly, it's Exall who features first, sketched in a few caricatured details as a 'bosomy

English rose' while Bowman is 'the friend in specs I could talk to'. This cartoonish pair represent two stereotyped opposites – one beautiful, sexualised and unattainable - the other unattractive but more approachable.

The American wit and writer Dorothy Parker, famous for her pithy wisecracks, once commented that 'men seldom make passes at girls who wear glasses', but clearly for Larkin – himself so short-sighted that he was deemed unfit for military service during the Second World War – the 'friend in specs' was the safer bet. Notice that relationships here are depicted as a kind of trial, a rite of passage that's definitely less than pleasant. The idiom Larkin uses is 'the whole shooting-match' – a phrase that carries overtones of conflict and competition, and also suggests that relationships are something of a chore. He is clearly out of his league – an idiom that he doesn't use, but could have – with the 'bosomy English rose' and therefore settles for second best, underlined by his use of end-focus as the first stanza reaches its conclusion. The impersonality of 'the friend' is telling: Bowman is defined by her relationship to Exall, rather than being a person in her own right.

A little less conversation

The most significant aspect of the relationship between Larkin and Bowman is the way that Larkin depicts it in terms of quantities and transactions, rather than emotions. Look how many references there are to numbers: 'about twenty years'; 'two girls'; 'seven years after that'; 'over four hundred letters'; 'gave a ten-guinea ring'; 'numerous cathedral cities'; 'I met beautiful twice'; 'about five attempts'; 'two snaps'. It's as if Larkin has kept a tally of what he has done and how much he has spent during the years he and Bowman were together. His focus is firmly on what *he* has done: he took her out, wrote her letters and gave her a ring. You can almost imagine him calculating what he must be owed in return. We imagine, perhaps, that he hope he's earnt some wild oats. If this makes Larkin seem resentful and miserly, then this is clearly a deliberate ploy, because he's not afraid to draw attention to his own inadequacy. There's a clear example of this at the end of the second stanza, when we're reminded that the 'bosomy rose' is not a fantasy figure glimpsed from afar, but a real presence who is therefore able to make Larkin perfectly aware of what she thinks of him. Larkin's statement that 'I believe / I met beautiful twice' is both succinct and brilliantly expressive, its mock-casual 'I believe' balanced by the dryness of 'beautiful'. Her mocking rejection of Larkin – 'She was trying / Both times [so I thought] not to laugh' – underlines his awareness that in her eyes, he is a faintly ridiculous figure. Poor Larkin: not only does *he* know that he isn't good enough for 'bosomy rose', but she does as well, and he knows that she does. If *Wild Oats* is a self-portrait, it's one that looks the poet's failings right in the eye.

Indeed, one of the saving charms of this most unromantic of love poems, emptied entirely as it is of the sometimes florid language of love, is Larkin's unflinchingly unromantic depiction of himself as a lover. He's nothing like a Romantic literary hero, such as Lord Byron, pictured opposite, or like a suave matinee idol of the time, such as Frank Sinatra. Larkin does not try to present himself as dashing or charming or handsome, or even witty. In fact, he's distinctly ordinary, humdrum and rather blokeish [he seems fixated on the rose's 'bosomy' charms]. The poet does not employ any sort of soft or flattering light; we feel he is being, in fact, honest about himself and his relationships. This is the honest, down-to-earth, sceptical Larkin that his friend Kingsley Amis described as demonstrating 'the scrupulous awareness of a man who refuses to be taken in by inflated notions of either art or life'. In this poem, Larkin, or his persona, refuses to be taken in by inflated or sugar-coated ideas about love and relationships.

The fact that he still remembers this meeting, from 'twenty' years back, and sees it as significant still, suggests this was the closest he ever actually got to 'sowing his wild oats', which could be seen as tragic or comic, or both. Perhaps there is a certain wry humour to the self-deprecating way Larkin depicts himself; in public the poet did seem to enjoy presenting himself as a rather glum, Eeyorish figure. Larkin excelled especially at writing about stunted, unfufilled lives, about characters who feel awkward and inadeqaute, including himself.

There's more inadequacy, for example, in the final stanza, which details the end of Larkin and Bowman's relationship. The poet depicts himself as entirely passive in this break-up, portraying it as a dispassionate, one-sided 'agreement / That I was too selfish, withdrawn / And easily bored to love'. Notice that he simply counters this judgement with a sour agreement that's also a dismissal: 'Well, useful to get that learnt'. There's a sense, really, that he knew this all along. [Larkin seems remarkably faithful to the truth here. When Bowman wrote to Larkin to end their relationship, she alluded to the sense of dissatisfaction and discontent that had clearly marked

Larkin's behaviour: 'I hope that you will be happy in Ireland and that you will, in a new environment, be able to come to better terms with life and with yourself'.]

There's a final sting. At the end of the poem, the narrator reveals that 'In my wallet are still two snaps / Of bosomy rose with fur gloves on'. These photographs – described by Andrew Swarbrick as 'the contraband of fantasy smuggled into the real world' – underline the gap between the unattainable and the reality, between what one would like and what one has to settle for. The poem's final line – 'Unlucky charms, perhaps' – is perhaps an admission that clinging to this fantasy blighted the poet's relationship with Bowman or other women more generally, that it's best to be happy with what you've got rather than hanker after something else. But the final hedge, 'perhaps' – a statement and not a question – suggests that if they *have* been unlucky charms, then Larkin doesn't really care.

Wild Oats Crunch

YEARS – GIRLS – BOSOMY – SPECS – SPARKED – SHOOTING-MATCH – EVER – BUT – SEVEN – LETTERS – RING – END – NUMEROUS – BELIEVE – BEAUTIFUL – LAUGH – PARTING – AGREEMENT – SELFISH – BORED – USEFUL – WALLET – ROSE – PERHAPS

Philip Larkin, *Talking in Bed*

All the lonely people

Have you ever heard the saying 'sometimes a crowded room can be the loneliest place on earth'? In **Talking in Bed**, Philip Larkin makes it clear that the very ordinary, universal experience of being in bed with another person can be a pretty bleak, lonely one. That's what you might expect from a poet who was described by his biographer Andrew Motion as being 'like a sexually disappointed Eeyore'. Larkin finished writing *Talking in Bed* in August 1960, ten years into his relationship with Monica Jones, a lecturer in English literature at Leicester University. He and Monica were still together at the time of his death in December 1985, but in the years in between, Larkin had relationships with a number of other women. In view of this, it's easy to interpret the poem as a straightforward reflection on the impossibility of being honest with the person you're supposed to be in love with, prompted by Larkin's own experience of love and its complications. After all, the poem's composed of ordinary, straightforward words and sounds like someone speaking, rather glumly. Actually, it's a very clever little lyric, and a fantastic example of what Larkin does so well, fusing imagery, metre and rhyme [or lack of it] so that every part of the poem helps to create a consistent whole.

Tempting as it is to see *Talking in Bed* as a reflection of Larkin's own situation, one important thing to notice about the poem is that it isn't about one particular couple at all. Look at the pronouns, or rather, the lack of them: there's no 'I' or 'she', no 'me' or 'you'. In fact, the only personal pronoun in the poem is 'us' – a pronoun that could refer to the 'us' of one specific  couple, but could also be extended to the 'us' of humanity in general. As the critic Andrew Swarbrick states, the poem is about a 'universal condition', in which an idealised image of happy relationships is replaced by sober awareness of how difficult it is to communicate with the person you're meant to be closest to.

It's so funny how we don't talk anymore

Talking in Bed begins straightforwardly enough, setting up an image of openness – 'An emblem of two people being honest' – that seems almost timeless. Notice, though, that Larkin starts to undercut this image in the very first line, with the modal verb 'ought': when we're in bed with someone, we should feel able to talk to them, but already we're introduced to the fact that this might not be the case. The pun at the beginning of the second line – 'Lying together' – continues to unsettle. The notional couple in the poem are 'lying' physically, in bed, but there's also the suggestion that they're not telling the truth. With each other, or with themselves? Both? Larkin doesn't specify, but the hint is there. The second stanza, with its opening 'Yet', reinforces the sense of discord. Intimacy is replaced by a lack of communication: 'more and more time passes silently'. The sibilants, that could be shushing and calming, are quietly troubling instead: something is clearly not right.

As the poem progresses, it continues to set off depth charges. Larkin controls these through his careful use of negation. Look, for instance, at the phrase 'The wind's incomplete unrest'. 'Complete unrest' would be understandable – a state of disturbance and disruption – but 'incomplete unrest' is more complex, suggesting something more awkward and perhaps intermittent. The wind is sometimes calm and settled, but sometimes it isn't. As an example of pathetic fallacy, the message conveyed by this image is clear. The dark towns that 'heap up on the horizon' – appearing from afar as in some time-lapse film – seem vaguely threatening because they are so impersonal, symbolising a hostile world that is utterly indifferent to the couple's plight.

The indifference of the outside world is expressed in the line 'None of this cares for us' – a line interpreted by the critic James Booth as 'a gesture of extravagant despair'. However, Andrew Swarbrick reads the line differently, arguing that 'this central moment in the poem is oddly consoling'. For Swarbrick, 'the wind expresses a universal condition of purposeless change', one in which 'relationships are inevitably fragile'. However, the wind actually serves to bring the couple together: even though they are unable to communicate with each other, they are nevertheless joined together by the wind's impersonal force, by the constant movement of the clouds.

Tripwires

The poem's final sentence presents what Booth describes as 'a series of verbal tripwires' for the reader. As with 'incomplete unrest', the reader has to disentangle the logic of what Larkin is saying. Take, for example, 'This unique distance from isolation'. If you are at a distance from isolation, then strictly speaking, you're close to someone – but what Larkin is actually presenting to us is a situation where we might be physically close to somebody, but isolated psychologically by our inability to communicate with them. Similarly, 'not untrue and not unkind' should logically mean 'true and kind', but instead it means something much more subtle. The only words the couple can find are not lies, and not unkindnesses – but they are not the wholehearted, honest declarations of truth and affection that might be expected of a couple who are close enough to be physically intimate.

This overriding sense of awkwardness supported by the poem's irregular metre and rhyming pattern. Its structure seems regular enough – four three-line stanzas – but dig a little deeper and you'll see that this regularity is built on very shaky foundations. Count the number of syllables in a line. Most lines have ten syllables – but there are elevens and nines in there as well, and the last two lines contain six and eight syllables respectively. Try to work out where the stressed syllables are, and there's even more irregularity. If you underline the stresses in the first stanza, for instance, you'll get something like the following:

'<u>Tal</u> / king / in / <u>bed</u> / <u>ought</u> / to / be / <u>eas</u>/ i /est,

<u>Ly</u> / ing / to / <u>ge</u> / ther / <u>there</u> / <u>goes</u> / <u>back</u> / so / <u>far</u>,

An / <u>em</u> / blem / of / <u>two</u> / <u>peo</u> / ple / be / ing / <u>hon</u> / est.'

Rather than having a regular metrical pattern [like iambic pentameter], the poem's metre shifts all over the place, not allowing you to settle into comfortable predictability. And look at the rhyming pattern. Larkin presents us with half-rhymes – 'easiest', 'honest' and 'unrest'; 'horizon' and 'isolation'. There's a sense of something that doesn't quite fit. Ironically, it's only as the poem reaches its close that we get full rhymes: a dawning realisation with 'sky' and 'why', and then the concluding triplet of 'find', 'kind' and 'unkind', presenting us with a statement that is offered up as a universal truth. [And notice how the stresses in that final line fall not on 'true' and 'kind', as they do in the previous line, but on the negative prefixes: 'not / un / true / and / not / un / kind.']

If you wanted any more proof of Larkin's negativity about love, look at the length of the poem. At twelve lines, it's almost fourteen – almost a sonnet, the poetic form that's supremely associated with love. The curtal sonnet – a curtailed sonnet, a sonnet cut short – is a form usually identified with the nineteenth-century poet Gerard Manley Hopkins, but two particularly important examples are *On My First Sonne* by Ben Jonson, a poem lamenting the death of his son at the age of seven, and *The Falling Leaves* by Margaret Postgate Cole, a poem written in 1915 about the deaths of thousands of young men in Flanders. Both of these curtal sonnets are about lives that end prematurely: it's easy to see why their authors chose this particular form. Is Larkin trying to suggest that love will never really match up to our expectations? We don't know whether the twelve lines of *Talking in Bed* were intended to gesture towards a truncated sonnet, but it's certainly an interesting way of interpreting this poem.

Talking in Bed crunched:

OUGHT – LYING – HONEST – YET – UNREST – CLOUDS – DARK – NOTHING – ISOLATION – DIFFICULT – WORDS – UNTRUE

Seamus Heaney, *Punishment*

What a curious love poem Heaney's **Punishment** is! It certainly does not conform to your typical treatment of love. Instead it is a murky archaeological dig into the past to comment on the present, a meditation on the difficulties of imposing individual morality on collective misbehaviour and a [slightly but not overly] guilty commentary on the role of the artistic voice in society. And all in just 44 lines too.

Love ties us together

The most striking first impression of the poem is its unusual shape on the page. The long[ish] sequence of 11 quatrains together with the notably short lines, which range from 2 to 8 syllables, give the impression of a compressed, dense flow of expression. In some ways the poem appears like the pressurised bog bodies that inspired the poem. In another more sinister connection to the poem the poem resembles a rope, taut with tension  between past and present, individual and collective, condemned and condemner, silence and voice. Unsurprisingly, the poem sees a number of oppositions interrogated by Heaney.

The lack of a rhyme scheme alongside the density of Heaney's observations [just look at all those nouns] makes each little quatrain surprisingly powerful. If it wasn't for the strong metre of the poem it would feel almost conversational. Heaney begins four of his eleven quatrains with the personal pronoun 'I' making it a deeply personal response. However, that strong personal voice is balanced by the notably silent 'you' of the bog body, who is imaginatively brought to life by Heaney before being even more imaginatively conflated with the present [or recent past of the Northern Irish civil conflict, euphemistically titled The Troubles].

Objectification and Objectivity

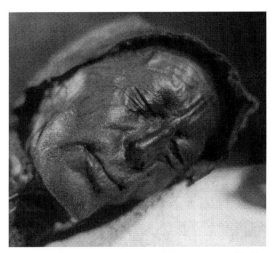

While the metaphor of digging remains most strongly linked with Heaney's autobiographical early poetry, the revelations arising from such excavations in this poem seems more cultural than individual; a social process that can lead to enlightenment. Eerily, the digging in the poem seems more focused on the hidden bringing itself to the surface as opposed to a deliberate excavation discovering the past. While the bog body is presented as passive, the past that comes with it takes on a much more active role. The utopian view of History as warning us about the mistakes of the past is problematised by Heaney as he suggests that no such lessons of improvement have been learned. Instead, European cultures are trapped in cycles of brutal tribal violence that destroy individual freedoms. Writing in 1973, and attacked by some critics as presenting a simplistic and pessimistic view of cultural conflict, the subsequent conflicts over the past 40 years have proven Heaney depressingly accurate.

However, Heaney firstly chooses to personalise the past by focusing on the victim of the punishment. The description here is quite sensual in capturing the vulnerability of the bog body suddenly exposed to the elements once again. Empathetically, the speaker 'can feel [...] the wind / on her naked front' and the description of how the wind 'shakes the frail rigging / of her ribs' emphasises further the delicacy of the female described. Heaney also uses the gentle alliteration of soft r-sounds together with the brittle short i-sounds in 'rigging' and 'ribs' to reinforce this fragility. This crafting of soundscapes is reflective of a wider strategy in the beginning stages of the poem. The first two stanzas are full of subtle sound patterns where a proliferation of soft n-, l- and s- sounds are subtly snagged on harsher fricatives and plosives. The n- sounds of 'can', 'nape', 'neck', 'wind', 'naked', 'front', 'nipples' are counteracted by the k-sounds in 'neck', 'naked' and 'shake' in particular. This conflict in sound connects to the wider issues of individual conflict with collective expectations in the poem.

The n-sounds are most noticeable in the alliteration of 'nape', 'neck',' 'naked' and 'nipples'. This sensual alliteration becomes increasingly erotic as the poem slides from neck to breasts [and further down] like a lover. This lovingness seems uncomfortable and the poem has drawn much feminist fire for its eroticising and objectification of the female form. Indeed the listing of the parts of the female recalls the Petrarchan lover's blazon. It could be argued that the patriarchal tribal justice that killed this woman in the past is matched by a similarly patriarchal reception in the present through the male speaking voice's objectifying observations. This objectification emphasises the fragility and weakness of the female can also be seen much later in the poem where Heaney describes the 'brain's exposed / and darkened combs' and the 'muscles' webbing'. Both 'exposed' and 'webbing' allude to the physical vulnerability of the woman's body whereas 'combs' suggests something that should not be exposed at all i.e. the honeycomb of a beehive.

The sensuality signalled by 'I can feel' at the start segues to greater objectivity where 'I can see' sees a subtle distancing from the body. The voice becomes more scientific in its archaeological observations, almost as if describing a crime scene. This change is again signalled sonically with a slowing down of the short lines through long, broad vowel sounds, such as 'dr<u>ow</u>ned', 'b<u>o</u>dy' "b<u>o</u>g', 'st<u>o</u>ne' as well as 'fl<u>oa</u>ting r<u>o</u>ds and b<u>ough</u>s'. Furthermore, the observations move from the particularities of the female body to the environment that housed it. Mention of 'the weighing stone', however, re-introduces the sinister suggestions of homicide [previously suggested by 'halter'] that can be easily forgotten in the sensuality of the opening.

May the road of the past rise up to meet you
A fusion of body with bog is suggested by Heaney when he describes the body as a barked sapling / that is dug up' in the fourth quatrain. 'Barked' describes the colouration of the body while 'sapling describes the woman's youth. The sound combinations of this phrase manage to capture the simultaneous brittleness yet great durability of the body where the crackling fricative of 'barked' runs both with and against the more elastic suppleness of

'sapling'.

Such skilful sculpting of sounds reappears in the final line of this quatrain where Heaney's description is most compressed. Like the great pressure of material pressing down on these bog bodies, the phrase 'oak-bone, brain-firkin' condenses meaning down to the absolute minimum words necessary. The power of this line can be seen in its relentless four sequential stressed beats. Heaney uses hyphenation to yoke bog to body and surrounds the subject with a casing of objects. The 'bone' and 'brain' of this woman are enveloped imaginatively by wood. 'Firkin' is one of those typically Anglo-Saxon sounding words that Heaney is so fond of in his poetry. It's a small wooden vessel for storing butter and here describes the woman's skull, which becomes literally a brain container. As mentioned, the sound patterns contained in this most condensed poetic line are impressive. Not only does Heaney employ assonance through the broad vowels of 'oak-bone' he links the 'bone, brain' through alliteration and the 'brain-firkin' through consonance. He also manages to connect the 'oak' and 'firkin' through the sharp fricatives of the k-sounds. The overall impression is a phrase meshing opposing concepts together through several sonic strands.

Love crime or hate crime?

While such nuanced sonic analysis is all very fine how exactly does Heaney's poem relate to love? The concept of love is disturbingly introduced into the poem via the noose around the woman's neck, which Heaney describes as 'a ring // to store / the memories of love'. This extraordinary equation of the noose and the wedding ring conflates murder and love, which allows the poem to reveal its central preoccupation: the collective 'punishment' of inappropriate love. Here the poem reveals the bog body as a 'little adulteress' who becomes a 'scapegoat' for the 'tribal, intimate revenge' of straying from expected norms. Conflict between the individual and the collective is revealed in the phrase 'before they punished you', where the faceless 'they' are subtly denigrated by the adjectives associated with the 'you' figure: 'little' and 'poor'. The fact that Heaney describes this woman as 'under-nourished' also reinforces her victimisation.

Again, from a feminist perspective the 'little adulteress' is alone; there is no male counterpart to be found suggesting that the female paid for a joint transgression. Describing this woman as a 'poor scapegoat' further emphasises the unjust brutality of her punishment, where 'scapegoat' implies her punishments is very much public and to be seen as a chastening deterrent to further transgressive behaviour. However, Heaney is not content for us to sympathise with this 'poor' victim of ancient pagan brutality.  Cleverly he connects it to the time of composition [early 1970s Northern Ireland] through the description of her 'tar-black face'. In the Northern Irish Troubles the Irish Republican Army [I.R.A.] publicly humiliated any Catholic women caught fraternising with members of the British army.

Women were 'cauled in tar' and 'wept by the railings'. The the use of 'tar' explicitly connects them to the 'tar-black' face of the 'little adulteress'. Heaney's verbification of the noun 'caul' is brilliantly appropriate and sinister. 'Caul' can mean close fitting woman's cap, but can also refer to where a new-born baby's head is covered by a part of the amniotic sac. Either way it denotes the tar cap forced on these women, but also connotes a terrible corruption of the innocent and defenceless. However, Heaney complicates such a straightforward reading when he describes the women as 'your betraying sisters'. Clearly, it is another explicit equation of past and present female victims but this is made problematic by the adjective 'betraying' as this suggests wrongdoing and guilt rather than victimisation and innocence. There is an implied criticism of the women's looking for love in all the wrong places. Love then must be seen not as an action between two individual but an action requiring social validation. There is also a suggestion of the vindictiveness of such 'tribal' justice with Heaney implying that these women [ancient and modern] are punished because they are 'beautiful' – a source of female power over men.

Past and present: Learning the wrong things from the right lessons?

This complication of the relationship between male observer and female observed dominates the end of the poem. Again, feminist critics rightly lament the silencing of the female victims who require a male voice to articulate their experiences. Additionally, it is not a straightforward moral warning about patriarchal oppression of natural female desires. Heaney conjures up a heady brew of sympathy and silence, powerlessness and protest that alludes to the role of the artist's voice in society.

The complex responses of the male speaker to the silent female is continued in the assertion that he 'almost' loves her. The possessive pronoun 'my' again reinforces the power of the individual male speaker but also the power of the patriarchal collective. The fact that he can only 'almost love' her prevents a simple presentation of the speaker as moral crusader. In fact he is much less than a voice of reason, a voice of moral outrage. Instead the poet is portrayed an 'artful voyeur; a sort of peeping tom who gains artistic power from observation but not through interaction. There is a worrying suggestion of the parasitic relationship between life and art as well as humanity and artist. Heaney admits his cowardliness when he proclaims rather than intervening to help the women, he would have cast 'the stones of silence'. This allusion to biblical stories of stoning, particularly Mary Magdalene for adultery, is highly effective as it introduces another male-voiced narrative that considers collective punishment of individual female wrongdoers. However, the fact that Christ prevents such brutality in this story slyly suggests another way forward...especially for a group supposed to be living by the teachings of Christ. A deep irony is presented by Heaney in the discrepancy between Catholic doctrine and Catholic nationalist behaviour. The sibilance of 'cast, I know / the stones of silence' powerfully creates a whispering effect that reflects the murmurs of disagreement that ultimately accept such 'tribal, intimate revenge'.

This individual weakness in the face of collective power is shamefully described in the discrepancy between moral lip service and practical bravery. Heaney admits how he would 'connive / in civilised outrage / yet understand the exact /and tribal, intimate revenge'. The artist would ultimately ignore this brutal victimisation of vulnerable young women through a type of hollow performative outrage. The terrible thing about this is that he is unable to make any meaningful gestures because he understands too well the logic behind such brutality. When he proclaims he has 'stood dumb' it creates a strong sense of self-loathing that captures the difficulties of making an individual protest in the face of collective actions. In one sense, actually writing such a poem makes the type of meaningful protest that many individuals are unable to make in reality. The artist ultimately says the things

that the individual cannot. However, as the rest of the poem highlights, Heaney is no moral crusader. The message is not that such things are simply wrong; it's that such things are wrong but will continue happening. As with all punishments we are encouraged to think about the relationship between crime and punishment: does the punishment fit the crime? In both cases alluded to in the poem, it would seem not.

Crunchiment

FEEL – HALTER – NECK – NAKED – NIPPLES – BEADS – FRAIL – RIBS – DROWNED – BOG – WEIGHING – RODS – UNDER – SAPLING – DUG – FIRKIN – SHAVED – BLACK – BLINDFOLD – NOOSE – STORE – MEMORIES – ADULTERESS – PUNISHED – FLAXEN-HAIRED – TAR-BLACK – SCAPEGOAT – ALMOST – CAST – SILENCE – VOYEUR – EXPOSED – DARKENED – WEBBING – BONES – DUMB – BETRAYING – CAULED – WEPT – CONNIVE – CIVILISED – UNDERSTAND – TRIBAL

Keith Douglas, *Vergissmeinnicht*

The tanks that broke the ranks

They say that the First World War was the first modern war. Certainly, it was the beginning of the end for traditional hand-to-hand combat, as rifles and bayonets and horses, the symbols of centuries of warfare, began to be replaced by long-range artillery, bomber planes, trenches, chemical attacks and tanks. But it was during the Second World War that the lethal potential and terrifying implications of the new species of impersonal and deathless mechanical weapons began to be fully recognised and exploited. This new ability to kill [or to be killed] remotely, without having to look the enemy in the eye and sense a shared humanity, meant that killing became yet more dispassionate, breeding a cynicism which built on the already-tarnished reputation of the 'glorious war'. The poets of the Second World War responded by producing a body of work which detailed their experiences in an impassive, unsentimental voice. And none was more unsentimental than Keith Douglas.

Douglas had completed his officer training at Sandhurst in February 1941 and, after a brief stint with the 2nd Derbyshire Yeomanry, had been transferred to the Sherwood Rangers, and posted first to Palestine and then to Egypt. Egypt was a key territory in the Western Desert campaign, and El Alamein, the site of a railway halt, was one of its most strategically important regions. It was there [as the name suggests] that the Second Battle of El Alamein took place: a brutal conflict with vicious encounters between opposing divisions of armoured vehicles, which cost the Axis around 50,000 men and 500 tanks in the three weeks of fighting, and the Allies some 14,000 and 400 of the same. On the third day of the battle, after disobeying an order to remain  behind, Douglas had led his tank division into the fray, and before long had been hit square by the shell of an anti-tank gun. It was a face-to-face encounter with death, and yet, remarkably, none of his crew was killed, and they managed to destroy the gun-pit before it could fire on them again.

Three weeks passed and the battle finished, and Douglas and his men returned 'over the nightmare ground' and 'found the place' where their tank had been hit. They found, too, the bloated and rotting corpse of the soldier who had attacked them unsuccessfully, and whom they had killed, sprawled in the shadow of his anti-tank gun. It was this experience that provided the narrative for **Vergissmeinnicht**, one of Douglas' most celebrated poems, and one in which he most powerfully evoked the desensitising effect of the new mechanical warfare.

Cleanin' my rifle [and dreamin' of you]

A key conceit for Douglas in capturing this cynicism and callousness is his blurring of the boundary between animate and inanimate, between flesh and blood and cold hard steel. As the soldiers are losing their humanity, Douglas seems to suggest, their weapons are gaining it. In the second stanza, for example, he personifies the 'frowning' barrel of the dead man's gun, ascribing it a human face with the vaguely displeased expression of the cartoon Army General: an expression whose indifference fails to convey the full horror of the blood-soaked scene. Later, Douglas has the adjective 'gunpit' qualify the unusual noun 'spoil', which can mean valuable items which have been pillaged or stolen, or the arms and armour of a slain enemy, but can also mean the uneaten remains of an animal carcass. Part of the effect here is in demonstrating that the poet has grown insensitive to death and suffering, and feels little guilt in dehumanising the dead German, reducing him to meat for scavengers to pick at. But part of the effect, again, is in breathing life into the inanimate steel: 'spoil' can be read as referring to the remnants of the destroyed 'gunpit', with the poet reimagining the ruined weapon as a dead and mutilated body, the machinery once more ascribed the attributes of a living creature.

Douglas extends this conceit when he describes how the dead soldier's lethal 'equipment' is 'mocking' the man who once operated it, attributing to the weapon the capability of human-to-human interaction. And when those two lines are read in full – 'mocked at by his own equipment / that's hard and good when he's decayed' – a sexual euphemism playing on 'equipment' and 'hard' becomes unmistakable. The lines provide more evidence of the cold-heartedness which the war has engendered in the speaker, in this case by recording the crude-ish joke he's made about a guy he's killed. But the image of the still-living weapon, unhurt and un-decayed, laughing at the frailty of the human body, also projects a vision of a world in which the machines have outlived their operators. Sex is a symbol of life, vitality and the continuation of the species, and is one of the fundamental interactions between humans. The dead soldier's 'decayed equipment' – his sexual impotency – therefore, reflects the broader demise of common human interaction, the loss of sympathy and sensitivity, and reads as a forecast of extinction.

There is a definite sense that the inanimate weapons have taken control of the soldiers' actions; that the soldiers have become more a tool of the weapons than vice versa. After all, 'mockery' isn't a balanced human interaction: it establishes a hierarchy which, in this instance, places the dead man's 'own equipment' above him. This reversed-ranking was hinted at in the poem's second stanza, where Douglas describes the barrel of the German's gun 'overshadowing' him – 'overshadow' can of course mean 'to cast a shadow over', but its other meaning of 'to diminish the relative importance of' is equally relevant here. And the peculiar simile, 'like the entry of a demon', in that  same stanza introduces a motif of demonic enchantment, as if the rise of mechanical weaponry has acted like an malicious spirit, possessing the soldiers and driving them to cruelty. It's a motif which seems to be continued in the poem's final stanza where, in the line 'And Death who had the soldier singled', Douglas appears to portray himself as the Grim Reaper [he killed the man, after all]. No wonder, then, that those still living feel distant and callous: they've lost their compassion, and they've surrendered control to the pitiless demon of war.

Don't let's be beastly to the Germans

In another of his poems, *Desert Flowers*, Douglas acknowledged his debt to the First World War poet, Isaac Rosenberg: 'Rosenberg I only repeat what you were saying'. But the narrative of *Vergissmeinnicht* is more reminiscent of a work by another Great War poet, Wilfred Owens, titled *Strange Meeting*. In that poem a soldier enters the underworld and meets an enemy soldier he had killed the previous day, just as Douglas returned and saw the man his crew had killed. Douglas' poem, though, is far more cynical and far less conciliatory than Owens', with the mutual respect and pity which the soldiers of *Strange Meeting* exhibit replaced by cruelty and derision and little success in taking a non-partisan view of the slaughter.

The gloating tone of the 'equipment' pun is far from the only instance of the speaker's mercilessness. He plays on the idiom 'with contempt' in the line 'We see him almost with content', simultaneously conveying the disdain the men feel towards the German and their delight in seeing him dead. He contrasts their nonchalant response with that of the dead man's lover who 'would weep', reinforcing the lack of tears with the image of the dry 'dust' on the 'paper eye', and seeming to revel in his breezy description of the swarming flies and the erupted belly. And he casts scorn on the signed photograph which they find among the soldier's possessions, a gift from his girlfriend back home, with the bathos of 'who has put' initiating the sneering tone, and the childish connotations of 'copybook' writing reinforcing it.

The adjective 'gothic' seems pointedly chosen, too: though it is commonly used to refer to the blackletter typeface often associated with written German, the word can also mean 'barbaric' or 'savage' or, most pertinently, 'in bad taste'. These alternative connotations serve to convey the speaker's feeling that the woman's gift too soppy and sentimental, and the Hollywood overtones of the carefully-placed 'script', coupled with the fact that

 *Vergissmeinnicht*, as well as being an expression and the name of a flower, was the title of a saccharine German love song from that era, certainly suggests that he thinks little of the sugar-coated romanticism on display. Moreover, the speaker seems determined to destroy any vestige of genuine emotion which the signed photograph may carry, insisting that it has been 'dishonoured' – there's a chance he means that it has been sullied by its proximity to death, but it seems more likely, considering the gloating tone elsewhere, that he means the girl has been dishonoured because her boyfriend lost the battle and got himself killed.

There is almost no honour paid to the dead throughout the poem, culminating in the final stanza which, despite its celebrated delineation of the soldier's twin identities, 'the lover and killer', reads more like a parody of

113

wartime oration than a heart-felt reflection on the complex cruelty of war. The self-consciously Latinate inversion of 'who had the soldier singled', placing the verb at the end, does some of the work; the knowing archaism of 'mortal hurt', borrowed perhaps from *Romeo and Juliet*, finishes the job. Indeed, there seems to be an attempt to deny the dead German any value at all: that curious pun, 'We see him almost with content', could also be read as 'We see him almost with meaning' or 'with substance', with the implication being, 'Almost, but not quite'. This is supported by a proliferation of words relating to things not being fully real or of full value: 'almost' and 'seeming' are self-explanatory; 'abased' can mean 'degraded' / 'humbled', and can be used as a synonym for when currency is debased; 'mocked' contains the root 'mock' which can mean 'imitation' or 'counterfeit'. The dead German is unreal, the girlfriend's suffering is unreal – it's hard to find meaning and value, it seems, in the middle of the War.

Down forget-me-not lane

And yet, in that line, 'We see him almost with content', there is the feeling that Douglas and his crew are trying to see the dead German as real and valuable, but are simply unable to do so. The foregrounded opposition between that line and 'But she would weep to see today' demonstrates that the speaker recognises that the matter is purely subjective, that his perception of the situation is bound to be biased. He is, perhaps, more enlightened than others in acknowledging that, really, the German's life was worth no less than his own, at least to some people. But he is not so advanced as to be able to shed his patriotism and ingrained hatred of the Hun. History is written by the winning side, as it is here, and the sense of history – or, more, the sense of regression – runs strongly through the poem.

There are the archaisms highlighted above, to which might be added 'combatants', 'dishonoured' [with its connotations of chivalry], 'gothic' [in the sense of 'Germanic'], 'spoil' and 'swart'. They are words of earlier confrontations, with the Goths, with the 'swarthy' fighters of the Ottoman Empire, in which honour could be won and lost, and the spoils of war were the ready reward. And now they have resurfaced, lost once but returned again, as the repetition of 'gone' and 'found' in the poem's first stanza implies. The weapons may be different, but the inability to avoid bloodshed which marks millennia human existence is just as powerful as ever. Douglas sees in the scene, and in his own reaction to the sight of the dead German, a powerful  hand dragging him back into the past, into the primitive 'cave' of the man's 'burst stomach', which recalls not only rudimentary human life, but Plato's allegory of enlightenment [and the lack of it]. The 'dust' on the dead man's eye isn't just the sand of the desert: it's a reminder of the repetition of history and the inevitability of death; the same dust as in T.S. Eliot's 'I will show you fear in a handful of dust'; the same dust as the Bible's 'you are dust, and to dust you shall return'.

Douglas is suffering from a painful contradiction: there are faint traces of sympathy for the dead man, most evident in 'nightmare', perhaps, or 'who had one body and one heart'; but he is unable to escape the machinations of the civilisation which would have him feel no pity for the enemy, and has found his powers of compassion blunted by the remoteness and lottery of mechanised warfare. The inconsistency of the rhyme scheme – which shifts between ABBA, ABAB and AABB – and the use of pararhymes, which clashes, for example, 'heart' and 'hurt', seem to be a poetic embodiment of this contradiction. The gesture towards a rhyme-pattern is an attempt to make coherence and lyricism from brutality; the 'failure' of the rhyme scheme is the triumph of savagery and cynicism.

Vergissmeinnicht crunched:

COMBATANTS – NIGHTMARE – AGAIN – SPRAWLING – FROWNING – OVERSHADOWING – TANK – DEMON – SPOIL – DISHONOURED – VERGISSMEINNICHT – COPYBOOK – GOTHIC – CONTENT – ABASED – MOCKED – HARD – WEEP – SWART – DUST – CAVE – MINGLED – BODY – DEATH – MORTAL

Tony Harrison, *Timer*

Poor Florrie Harrison. A working-class housewife from Leeds, she must have been deeply proud when her clever son Tony won a scholarship to Leeds Grammar School and then went on to the University of Leeds to study Classics. Yet she was shamed by the explicit language in his first poetry collection *The Loiners*, exclaiming – as Harrison has recounted on a number of occasions – You weren't brought up to write such mucky books! Heaven knows what she'd have made of this poem, in which Harrison lists her underwear and intimate parts of her body. **Timer** is definitely not a conventional elegy. Nevertheless, in its own unusual, poignant way, it still manages to convey Harrison's love for his mother, confronting what has happened to her physical remains as the poet contemplates the passing of time.

 *Timer* is one of a series of poems that Harrison wrote about his parents after the deaths of his mother, in 1976, and his father, four years later. Many of these poems explore the gap that opened up between Harrison and his parents as a result of his education. There's a great example of this in another poem, *Book Ends*, in which Harrison describes the tension between himself and his father after his mother's death:

'Back in our silences and sullen looks,

for all the Scotch we drink, what's still between 's

not the thirty or so years, but books, books, books.'

Harrison has said that he wanted to write about his parents in ordinary language, using the kinds of words they themselves would understand. Nevertheless, we can also see, in *Timer*, how Harrison is showing off his ability as a poet. There's a strict rhyming pattern – ABAB – that persists through polysyllables such as 'St James's' and 'names is', 'incinerator' and 'together, later', and even through numbers – 'the son' and '6-8-8-3-1'. This cleverness prevents any potential slide into sentimentality [at some points it even sounds quite jaunty and even comical]. And significantly, while Harrison called this sequence of poems 'sonnets', they have neither the same rhyming pattern as traditional sonnet-sequences such as those by Shakespeare or Petrarch, nor even the same number of lines. Rather than the conventional fourteen lines, Harrison's sonnets have sixteen: they are 'caudate sonnets', from the Latin cauda, 'with a tail'. It's as if Harrison always has to have the last word.

The new normal

Timer conveys the feeling many people experience in the aftermath of bereavement, when things that in other circumstances would seem morbid or shocking become part of a 'new normal'. The first few days are swathed in a numbness that allows you to function while the bureaucracy of death – arranging funerals and sorting out paperwork – is dealt with. Thus Harrison's mother's death is described in terms of the banalities of officialdom, in the 'standard urn' that contains his mother's ashes and the 'envelope of coarse official buff' in which he is given her wedding ring. Some poems would treat this impersonality as a callous reflection on the insignificance of individual lives, but Harrison simply seems to accept it: the fact that his mother is reduced to a number, rather than being referred to by name, is registered without comment. [Compare this with W.H. Auden's poem *The Unknown*

Citizen, which offers a completely different take on the depersonalising effects of modern society]. Harrison is even able to confront the reality of what has happened to his mother's body. The references to 'gold', 'fire' and heat in the first line could quite easily belong to a conventional and rather pedestrian love poem. Here, however, the heat is not that of love but of the incinerator in which his mother is being cremated.

However, though it is understated, it would be a mistake to assume that emotion and specifically grief is absent from the poem. In their own ways those simple, unassuming adjectives, 'standard' and 'coarse', and the rough material 'buff', convey the poet's emotional rawness.

The second quatrain gives us a glimpse of the relationship between Harrison's parents, and of his father's simple, trusting faith in an afterlife. Harrison's father wanted his wife to be cremated with her wedding ring, a symbol of eternity that represents 'his surety that they'd be together, "later"'. Notice the way that 'later' acts as a euphemism here, as if Harrison's father  can't quite bring himself to speak of death itself. [And note, also, the intimacy of 'Dad']. Harrison himself passes no comment on this, but this lack of comment can itself be seen as an indication that the poet does not share his father's simple faith.

Harrison's own engagement with his mother's death is presented not in terms of any kind of spiritual reflection, but in much more practical terms. It's Harrison, for instance, who 'signed for the parcelled clothing as the son' and has to deal with the clerk who refers to his mother as a number, not a name. There's a clash, however, between the impersonality of the phrase 'the parcelled clothing' and the listing of the clothes themselves, their personal and even private nature being underlined by Harrison's use of colloquialisms: 'the cardy, apron, pants, bra, dress'. And notice also how Harrison's use of the definite article 'the', rather than the possessive pronoun 'her', creates a certain awkward distancing in 'the parcelled clothing', 'the son' and 'the cardy'. It's as if his mother's death is still raw and unfamiliar, his relationship with her not yet shifted into a new reality.

As the poem nears its end, the immediacy of 'now' brings us into a present in which Harrison confronts his mother's death more directly. The bureaucracy of death is replaced with the tactile intimacy of Harrison's 'warm palm' and the feeling of his mother's ashes sifting through her wedding ring – 'head, arms, breasts, womb, legs' – in a list that parallels that earlier listing of her clothes. It's significant that along with her head and limbs, Harrison chooses those parts of his mother's body associated with childbearing and nurturing [as opposed to, say, her lungs and liver]. As his mother's ashes slip through the circle of her wedding ring, Harrison offers us an image of physical closeness, of touch, between mother and son at the end: 'like that thing / you used to let me watch to time the eggs'. His mother's ashes are like the sand that runs through an egg-timer, an image that conjures up a powerful sense of inevitability. The adult son's reflection on the passing of his mother's life is thus bound up with a very brief memory of his childhood, of being allowed to do something that was special but at the same time very ordinary: one of those tiny moments that sums up a whole relationship, touched upon in a way that's all the more powerful because it's so fleeting.

 <u>Is _Timer_ a love poem?</u> Obviously, it's not about romantic love, and as a depiction of filial love – the love of a child for his or her parents – it is certainly unusual. After all, how many other poems have you read in which the narrator describes his mother's ashes, imagining which parts of her body they once were? Nevertheless, the poem is also unexpectedly tender. The image of the ashes running through the wedding ring could be seen as an echo of the moment of birth – an intense, personal moment uniquely shared by mother and son. Harrison's use of the present tense means that the poem ends on a note of contemplation: as readers, we are left holding our breath, witnessing a son adjusting to the fact that his relationship with his mother has now entered a new phase.

Timer crunched:

GOLD – ASHES – ENEVELOPE – WEDDING – DAD – INCINERATOR – ETERNITY – TOGETHER – SON – CARDY – CLERK – STILL – WARM – FEEL – THROUGH – USED

NB

Tony Harrison has written powerfully about the issues of class and education and of how he has felt like an interloper in the middle class world of poetry, describing himself as 'occupying' poetic space. If the literary canon is generally white, male and middle class, so its cultural artefacts can be seen as embued with the values of this privileged segment of the population. For female, non-white and working class poets adopting the form of a sonnet could therefore be seen as a sort of cultural selling out. Unsurprisingly then, Harrison like other non-DWM poets, tends to adapt traditional poetic forms, knocking them about a little to colonise and claim them as their own.

Carol Ann Duffy, *The Love Poem*

Borrowed lines

Reading this poem for the first time might be an oddly familiar experience. What is it about this poem that echoes something we have already read or heard? Looking carefully at **The Love Poem**, it is possible to find lines taken from other well-known texts. Take, for example, 'my mistress eyes' and 'let me count the ways' in the first stanza of the poem, which derive from famous love poems by William Shakespeare and Elizabeth Barrett Browning. In this opening twelve-line stanza Duffy quotes Shakespeare, Browning and Walter Scott. Attending to the following two stanzas reveals further literary sources: Thomas Wyatt, Philip Sidney, Thomas Campion, John Donne, Percy Bysshe Shelley and *The Song of Solomon*. On first reading, Duffy's poem is a sort of riddle designed to delight English teachers, or perhaps a literary site-seeing trip, on which the reader has to try to spot the quotations from famous poems. To some extent, Duffy's use of hyphens and form on the page helps the reader to identify which parts of the poems are quotes, but her decision not to use quotation marks means that they often blend into Duffy's own writing and are difficult to spot. On first impressions then, we might think that this is also a blatant case of plagiarism or Duffy just showing-off. But, actually *The Love Poem* is an ingenious version of a form of poem called a cento, a collage-type poem composed from the lines of other poems.

Does it matter that it is not 'A Love Poem', but 'The Love Poem' [emphasis added]? The use of this definite article, alongside Duffy's use of quotations, suggests a certain amount of self-reflexivity: this is a poem that considers the archetypal love poem often associated with poets like Sidney and Donne. The fact that Duffy uses one of the most recognisable quotations in the opening lines indicates that she isn't trying to cover up these stolen fragments of text. Shakespeare's famous line from *Sonnet 130* – 'my mistress' eyes' – placed in the very first lines of Duffy's poem – draws attention to the 'intertextual' quality of the poem.

'Intertextuality' refers to the relationship between texts and the meaning or effect generated by this relationship. Closer analysis of which texts Duffy has chosen to include in *The Love Poem* and the way in which she has employed these help us to pursue an intertextual approach. Is she quoting them to approve their sentiments, celebrate their wisdom about love or in admiration of their lyricism? Or is this audacious juxtaposition of great writers alongside Duffy's own writing more critical, or parodic even? These are questions we will go on to consider.

As Duffy cites a range of texts, it is perhaps simplest to begin by thinking about the nature of the quotations. Firstly, many of the quotations directly speak of love, desire and beauty in a rather lyrical manner: 'dear heart,/ how like you this' or 'look in thy heart/and write'. These lines belong to Thomas Wyatt and Philip Sidney. Whilst it might not be necessary to know everything about their writing, it is useful to consider the influences and literary eras in which these writers were a part. Writing in the sixteenth and seventeenth century, Wyatt and Sidney were influenced by Francesco Petrarch, an Italian poet whose sequence of sonnets called the Canzoniere expressed a romanticised, idealised love. Shakespeare, whilst also influenced by Petrarch, often countered the idealisation of love: as he writes *in Sonnet 130, My*

Mistress' eyes are nothing like the sun. With these thoughts in mind, we can consider how these quotations are deployed in Duffy's own lines. The opening of the poem, for example:

> 'Till love exhausts itself, longs
>
> for the sleep of words –
>
> > my mistress' eyes –
>
> to lie on a white sheet, at rest'

From the very first line of the poem love does not seem to be romantically portrayed. Rather, love is 'exhausted'. 'Exhausted' means extremely tired, but also worn out, spent, used up. This image is developed by Duffy's use of

Shakespeare's line as 'my mistress eyes' are described 'at rest' on a 'white sheet'. Shakespeare might have countered Petrarch's idealised sense of love in *Sonnet 130*, but Duffy takes this a step further. Whilst 'sheet' might be interpreted as the page, the phrase 'at rest' has associations with death. Indeed, this understanding of love not only as a fatigued entity, but as an entity on its deathbed, is further supported by the way Duffy uses Browning's line from *Sonnet 43*.

Looking at *Sonnet 43* provides context as to how Duffy is manipulating Browning's line. After all Browning writes 'How do I love thee? Let me count the ways' [and goes on to list those ways at some length] whereas Duffy sharply contrasts this lyrical abundance with 'or shrink to a phrase like an epitaph'. Duffy's simile underlines the previous associations with death by evoking a gravestone. Furthermore, internal rhyme further emphasises Duffy's point. By rhyming 'ways' and 'phrase', Duffy undermines Browning's romantic, abundant expression with her own rather more diminished representation of love. Given the way Duffy deploys these first few quotations, love in The Love Poem already appears not to be a romantic entity or an ecstatic pronouncement of emotion; instead it's presented as an exhausted, lifeless thing.

The forms of love

It is becoming apparent that Duffy uses the quotations in order to contest their idealised depictions of love. This challenge to traditional expressions of love in canonical love poetry is echoed in her use of form. What might be most apparent from initially looking at the poem is the way in which it moves across the page: many of the lines are indented from their otherwise left-hand margin, creating a rather jagged appearance on the page. Looking at this aspect of the poem more closely reveals that it is the quotations that are indented. The way Duffy has arranged her own lines against her borrowed ones creates a movement back and forth upon the page. The poem's form might be compared to a dialogue, which seems fitting for the argument she is making. It is significant how Duffy breaks these borrowed lines. Indeed, these lines are split differently in Duffy's poem than they are in their original form. In the second stanza, for example, she quotes Thomas Wyatt's poem They Flee from Me: 'dear heart,/ how like you this?' Duffy's enjambment of these lines creates a poem that emphasises the collage-like quality of her own poem: its patching and mixing of old and new lines. Developing this interpretation, we might look at how Duffy's splitting of quotations manipulates the rhythm of the original poems and therefore prompts us into new readings of old works. The lulling iambic metre of Wyatt's line is disrupted. Instead of stressing 'dear heart, how like you this?' Duffy's enjambment creates an abrupt, staccato pattern.

Despite its ragged appearance upon the page, *The Love Poem* has a consistent structure. Three twelve line stanzas, each beginning 'Till', allow Duffy to develop her less than positive take on love and love poetry. Pursuing the first stanza's associations of love with exhaustion and death, Duffy goes on to write:

> 'Till love gives in an speaks
> in the whisper of art –
>
> > dear heart,
> how like you this? –
> love's lips pursed to quotation marks
> kissing a line'

Reading this stanza in the context of the first one, gives us further understanding of how love in *The Love Poem* might be considered dead. After all, this is not quite  death as we know it. As Duffy explains in the poem's opening, this death occurs on the page, in the 'sleep of words'. What happens when these words are read? Does love come alive? Not quite. Duffy describes the repetitive quality of love in *The Love Poem*. Instead of saying anything new, love's lips are 'pursed to quotation marks'. Rather than love being lively and passionate, love says the same thing, over and over again. Whilst a traditional love poem might describe lips pursed to kiss the beloved, Duffy's poem describes love's lips 'kissing a line'. Evoking an inward-looking, perhaps self-regarding love that, lying on the page, has forgotten its real, physical origin and therefore seems deathly, Duffy parodies the love poem. As she goes on to quote Philip Sidney's *Loving in Truth*, [from his *Astrophil and Stella* sonnet sequence], the parody continues. Sidney's command 'look in thy heart/and write' represents a challenge to poetry that is disconnected from emotion. Whilst Duffy and Sidney would seem to have something in common here, Duffy uses this quotation to create further contrast as she goes on to write of 'love's light fading, darkening,/ black as ink on a page'. Even if a writer looks 'in thy heart' in order to write about love, as soon as love is written down it begins to fade and lose its vitality. The self-conscious act of writing does not capture or honour or celebrate love, but kills it.

Duffy's argument on love continues as, in the third and final stanza of the poem, we find that love is no longer in the heart, but 'all in the mind'. Traditionally, the heart and the mind have been understood to oppose one another: the heart is a symbol that represents passion, instinct and emotion, whereas the mind symbolically represents reason, rationality and intellect. Moreover, there is a disparaging tone to the phrase 'all in the mind' as it implies that something has been imagined when it does not actually exist. This idea – that love has no physical reality, but only endures on the page or in the literary mind – comes to a climax as the poem continues:

'O my America!

my new-found land –
or all in the pen
in the writer's hand – '

Here Duffy splits a line from John Donne's poem, To His Mistress Going to Bed: 'O my America! / My new-found land'. As with the other intertextual references, looking at Donne's poem helps us to get a better grasp of Duffy's. To His Mistress Going to Bed finds Donne touching his mistress' body and comparing such an act to the conquest of unexplored countries. Writing in the sixteenth-century, Donne would have understood America as an unmapped country. Whilst this conquest suggests a sense of adventure that is supported by Donne's excited exclamation 'O...!', Duffy contrasts Donne's lines with her own: 'or all in the pen / in the writer's hand'. As in the first stanza, Duffy's rhyme between 'land' and 'hand' emphasises the distinction she is making. Love might be expressed as an adventure in Donne's poem, but in Duffy's poem love is confined to the pen and controlled by the 'writer's hand'. Duffy follows with an example of the 'writer's hand' by quoting yet another text, this time the Song of Solomon.

> 'behold, thou art fair –
>
> not there, except in a poem,
>
> known by heart like a prayer,'

Whilst the biblical context of The Song of Solomon might seem inconsistent with Duffy's previous choices, the text is known for its celebration of sexuality and intimacy through its portrayal of two lovers. The commanding nature of the language ['behold'] is comparable to the previous command 'Look in thy heart' noted in Sidney's line, as well as Donne's 'O...!'In keeping with Duffy's less positive spin on love, the quotation from The Song of Solomon is also undermined. Echoing previous examples, Duffy employs rhyme to lend emphasis to her point. Following 'thou art fair', Duffy's simple, pared back language bluntly contradicts, and states otherwise: 'not there, except in a poem'. Resonating with her earlier descriptions of love as 'all in the mind' or 'in the pen', here we find love having no presence outside of the poem. The comma placed in this line creates a caesura, a pause, which increases the startling quality of the revelation and draws attention to the stark, austere reality of love's [and love poetry's] limitations.

The desire of the moth

However, a rather different, more mysterious tone is introduced to the poem by Duffy's simile. Whilst the idea of love 'known by heart like a prayer' resonates with previous descriptions of love as exhausted and repetitive – of 'love's lips pursed to quotation marks' – it might also provide a more hopeful tone. If love is like a prayer and prayers are used to address God, or another deity, then perhaps love is out there. Its existence, perhaps, depends on whether or not we believe in it. This uncertainty about love is underlined in the final four lines:

'both near and far,
near and far –
 the desire of the moth
for the star.'

The repetition and brevity of these lines allows us a chance to meditate on love's seemingly intangible existence, before Duffy concludes the poem on a line by the Romantic poet, Percy Bysshe Shelley. Borrowing Shelley's description of 'the desire of the moth / for the star' brings us to think about uncertainty as 'desire'. Thinking about where this line comes from in Shelley's work helps us to further examine Duffy's meaning. After all, Shelley's line comes from his poem *One Word is Too Often Profaned*. Given the nature of Duffy's poem, it's no surprise to learn that the word 'too often profaned' is love. Shelley finds this word overused and, most importantly, misused. Compared to other examples of intertextuality in Duffy's poem, crucially this citing from Shelley is not challenged, undermined or parodied. Instead it quietly enriches her point. Like the moth to the star, we continually search for love, even if it isn't attainable. Duffy's use of rhyme here similarly contrasts with previous examples: instead of emphasising contrast, 'far' and 'star' complement each other and consequently give us a greater sense of love as distant, uncertain, mysterious.

Having analysed the poem, how might we characterise it in terms of genre and how might the poem's conclusion prompt further interpretation? As noted earlier, there are elements of parody in *The Love Poem*. Throughout the text, Duffy undermines canonical literary expressions of love and portrays, instead, a rather less positive, less confident take on love. Given that so many of the writers quoted from are male, this parody might be understood as gender-driven. As a woman, Duffy is contesting men's portrayal of love. Given the deathly associations of love shrunken 'to a phrase like an epitaph' the poem also has an elegiac quality. After such critical representations of love, it might seem surprising that the poem ends on a slightly softer note about desire: Duffy concluding the poem with Shelley's quotation and not seeking to challenge it. However, look again at the poem's structure and it becomes possible to see how this thought on desire has been anticipated all along. As pointed out previously, each stanza begins with 'Till'. The repetition of 'Till' might be defined as 'anaphora': the repetition of words at the beginning of successive clauses. 'Till' is a subordinate conjunction and, in most cases, it will be followed by a main clause to complete a sentence. However, this main clause never arrives in Duffy's poem. As a result, the poem seems unresolved. As with the representation of desire in the final stanza, the whole poem might be read as a longing after love. Although love seems exhausted, restricted to the page and perhaps a figment of the imagination, does that stop us from yearning for it? Consequently, despite its parodic and elegiac elements, it is possible to interpret Duffy's poem as a true love poem. Duffy's conclusion drops any previous sense of parody to speak directly about love itself and its contradictory qualities.

The Love crunch:

EXHAUSTS – WORDS – MISTRESS – REST – LANGUAGE – COUNT – SHRINK – COME – ME – SYLLABLES – POOL – THEE – LOVE – WHISPERS – HEART – HOW – LIPS – KISSING – HEART – WRITE – DARKENING – INK – GARDEN – FACE – LOVE – AMERICA – NEW-FOUND – PEN – WRITERS – BEHOLD – EXCEPT – PRAYER – BOTH – AND – MOTH – STAR

Paul Muldoon, *Long Finish*

Mixed marriages

Dip a tentative toe into academic criticism of the poetry of Paul Muldoon and you'll discover some common threads, to use an appositely mixed metaphor. Critics comment on his 'conjunctions' and 'collisions', his 'striking mixtures' and 'fruitful misalliances' and laud the fundamental 'hybridity' of both his style and his themes. They focus too on Muldoon's 'radical formal experiments' with conventional and traditional poetic forms, noting approvingly his bravuara 'dexterity' with rhyme [he is sometimes said to be a poet who can even rhyme 'cat' with 'dog']. Muldoon's ironic wit, allusive playfulness and 'ludic verbal talents' are also oft-celebrated. Alarmingly, the difficulty of actually understanding his poems also crops up regularly, although disguised a little within academic discourse:

'Wily and mischevious...[his] conjunctions are energetic displays of a subtle, learned and ironic intelligence, placing the reader in a constant state of interpretive alertness and insecurity' [7]

---

[7] Hamilton and Noel-Todd, *The Oxford Companion to Modern Poetry*, p.434

Yikes, that doesn't sound attractive, especially if you'll got an A-level to teach / pass. For good measure, Justin Quinn in *The Cambridge Introduction to Modern Irish Poetry, 1800-2000* also finds that he's sometimes not quite sure what Muldoon is saying: Quinn refers to how Muldoon's characteristic shifts between 'faux naivetie and real naivety' often leave 'the reader unable to judge the import of what's being said'.[8] [Like the shift into the third person there, Justin.]

So, we can expect a Muldoon poem to:

1. mix together eclectic elements
2. shift between different tones [but be governed by the keynote of irony]
3. put a fast and loose new spin on an old, traditional form, re-booting, revamping and souping it up
4. feature complex and virtuosic rhyming
5. employ obscure / learned words and allusions
6. be darned difficult to understand.

Stephen Fry has written that managing the ballade rhyme scheme, with only two rhymes to spin out over 28 lines, may well be 'a doddle in French' but that it is the 'very bastard son of a mongrel bitch in English'[9]. Survey the Muldoon criticism for a moment and you won't be surprised to discover that not only is his poem **Long Finish** the very bastard son of a mongrel bitch, i.e. a ballade, it is, in fact, a more than double bastard son of a mongrel bitch, a

[8] *The Cambridge Introduction to Modern Irish Poetry*, 1800-2000, p. 178
[9] Stephen Fry, *The Ode Less Travelled*, p.244

more than double ballade. Now that's just showing off, surely. And, seriously, that is what some of Muldoon's sterner critics think of his poetry.

Mashed-up

Long Finish certainly mixes a number of different, seeminlgy disparate elements and holds them together through the poem's closed form. The title, for instance, according to Muldoon at least, alludes to a phrase beloved by wine producers and drinkers to describe a wine whose flavour lingers in the mouth. A number of other references to wine include to American 'Simi' chardonnay and the 'pure drop' of the final stanza. Added to this poetic wine we have references to a Japanese Noh play, *Matsukaze*, and its characters, to skin diseases, such as ezcema, and a prescription drug to treat it, Accutane, as well as stanzas about The Troubles in Northern Ireland, all wrapped up in a supposedly love poem to Muldoon's wife.

Words and phrases are drawn from a wide range of cultures, contexts and languages. My dictionary tells me that 'chuppah', for instance, is Jewish, 'Schloss' German and 'Triestine' is presumably Italian. Indeed one of Muldoon's more obscure words 'marhpane' eludes the dictionary entirely. [The closest is 'marchpane' which apparently is a Tudor type of marzipan. Turns out this is a typo and it should, indeed be 'marchpane'] 'Thou' is obviously archaic and 'and then some' modern colloquial. Muldoon also uses the more formal language of teaching: 'For the double of 'pine'/ is much the same in Japanese as English'. At other times he employs self-consciously poetic phrasing such as the paradox: 'bitter-rapture...blissful rows'. And there is too, running like a vein through the poem, the more erotic, sensual language that focuses intimately on his wife's body: 'your one bare / shoulder'; 'the veer of your neckline'; 'your breast'; 'your waist', on all of which he has 'designs'.

If we're dislocated linguistically and in danger of feeling insecure, sense of place does not come solidly to our aid. Nominally we are in a pinewood, but as well as the German chateau, the Schloss, and reference to Italian Trieste and Japanese drama, the poem enfolds references to a place of 'heather and mountain air' and specifically to small villages in Northern Ireland, 'Beragh and Sixmilecross'. In fact, decentred, we seem to be some kind of all over the place – where words and worlds collide, only in a good way.

New spins, new connections

First off, we'll have to acknowledge not only does Muldoon manage the ballade form [that bastard son etc. etc.] but that he more than doubles it. In fact he almost triples it. Conventionally the ballade consists of three eight line stanzas rounded off with a four line 'envoi', addressed to a prince. Long Finish either has nine stanzas followed by a double envoi or ten stanzas. Trace any of the end-rhymes words and you'll have to admit that the poem demonstrates a spectacular talent for managing rhyme. The second rhyme word, for instance. 'boughs' is rhymed with 'vows', 'thou', 'allows', 'the Dow' [The Dow Jones Index, i.e. the American stock exchange], 'sloughs', 'somehow', 'rows', 'cows', 'eyebrows', 'nows', 'souse', 'house', 'soughs', 'blouse', 'rouse' and 'espouse'. To pull that off and for the lines to make sense is impressive, but when you consider that the few rhymes sounds Muldoon has to play have to be recycled just as extensively and you have to take your hat off to the man. Muldoon doesn't just pump up the ballade form, he also knocks it about a bit, adding some bells and whistles - a few more rhymes, running two ballade rhyme patterns through alternating stanzas, finishing with a double envoi whammy, relocating the requisite Prince and so forth. But is this dazzling display of formal agility anything more than than showing-off?

Justin Quinn suggests an answer when he says that Muldoon's rhyming in general serves a thematic purpose: 'it reassembles the letters of words into new objects' and so 'insists in an oblique way on the extra-poetic values of wandering and surprise, of the rejection of grand narratives'.

Sonically, _Long Finish_ presents us with a dense mesh of interconnections running alongside the apparently disparate material, yoking it together. These repititions of words and sounds suggest the loops and twists of thought itself as well as the intermingly of the past with the present. Words and phrases appear in new contexts as the poem progresses, taking on different meanings, most notably the refrain-like end lines of each stanza. Another example is the image of the wine class filled as 'high as deceny allows' from the opening which reappears at the poem's end, modifed into the neckline 'as low as decency allows'. These devices embody hybridity into the core of the poem - repetition as well as change, continuity as well as development. Similarly, the poem also returns to the word and image of eczema after the apparent topic diversion into The Troubles.

A constant state of alertness and insecurity
Making sense of Muldoon's poem is indeed hard. Despite what we've just

said, in terms of meanings, the various aspects appear to pull in different directions and they're hard to resolve into a coherent whole. It's difficult to escape the feeling that really all these things - the Noh drama and the American wine - the German Chateau and the Irish farmer - the poet's marriage and the semi-automatic guns, are 'misalliances' that don't have much in common; that it is only the poem's form and soundscape, plus the repeating of key words, such as 'vows' and 'pine', that lend this rag bag a veneer of coherence.

Muldoon uses the phrase 'brings to mind' to link the most apparently disparate elements. To which a reader might respond, only to his rather loose and free-wheeling mind. The most striking example of this chraracteristic sort of hard-to-imagine conjunction is his wife's eczema patch which somehow reminds the poem not of a chateau [itself improbable] but, shockingly, of a 'trench' where two terrorists await their victim. At first this does seem like a rather far-flung, improbable even absurd analogy, tipping the poem precipitously into entirely diifferent territory. It could be argued, however, that both the patch and the trench share the fact that they are almost invisible; the eczema is 'all-but-cleared-up', while the trench is 'covered with pine boughs'. The worlds of love and of warfare share too the references to 'pine' and to 'vows', further grappling the misaligned images together. Notice too how the casual, almost jaunty phrase 'and then some' takes on a very different tone and meaning here, but is apposite. But what is this interlude about the Northern Ireland Troubles doing in a love poem? Isn't it simply out of place?

Again we might turn to the critics and specifically to Justin Quinn who writes that Muldoon 'refuses to deal with the issue of paramilitary violence in the

137

terms set by politics: the violent scenes appear incidentally in more wide-ranging and surreal narratives' [10]

And, though Muldoon may have escaped to the USA, such things were and are apart of his life and its contexts. Isn't it arguable that the fact that this image and dark memory springs to mind even within a love poem is all the more evidence for the pervasive influence of Northern Ireland politics? And of the shadow of the past on the present? That it is part of the essential darkness that defines the light for Muldoon?

The last stanza of this dazzling poem addresses Muldoon's wife and asks her to give up on the idea of trying to refine all the poem's material, reduce its 'dross' into something finer. That would be a pointless task, the poem says, embracing all its disparate, chaotic elements - all we can do is live life fully, with 'force' and 'fervour'. A traditional sentiment then at the end of an innovative, unconventional love poem.

[As this is an exceptionally long poem instead of reducing it to one word per line we've chosen one or two words or phrases from each stanza.] *The Long Finish* crunch:

WEDDING VOWS – DESIGNS – RAPTURE – ROWS – NECKLINE – MARKS AND HOODS – OPENING FIRE – LAND MINE – SALT – PINE – LONGING – LOSS – BLOUSE – REFINE – ROUSE – FERVOUR – AND THEN SOME

---

[10] *The Cambridge Introduction to Modern Irish Poetry*, p.178-179

NB

Type Paul Muldoon's name alongside the word 'postmodernism' into google and surprisingly little comes up. Neither is postmodernism a term used by Justin Quinn about Muldoon. Consider, however, the extent to which *Long Finish* exemplifies features of postmodernist literature, such as:

- the depiction of shifting identities through the mixing of genres
- the foregrounding of interxtextual elements, such as parody, allusion and pastiche
- the revisiting of the past with irony
- a tendency towards hybridity
- a preference for fragmentary and discontinuous narratives.

And doesn't Muldoon's poem exist in just the kind of disorientating space conceputalised by postmodernists as a 'decentred universe' where it's impossible to distinguish up from down, inside from outside and background from foreground? And it's a liberating space too, a space for Muldoon's ludic play? Thought so.

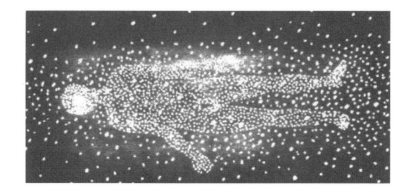

Michael Symmons Roberts, *To John Donne*

Oh my America!

'Intertextuality' refers to the relationships bewteen texts and the meaning or effect generated by these relationships. The title of Roberts' poem and various references within it highlight the way this poem draws on and is in a sort of literary dialogue with the earlier poet's *To My Mistress Going to Bed*. The metaphysical poet Donne's work is a seduction poem, boldly encouraging his object of desire to unclothe herself so that the libidinous poet can let loose his 'roving hands' to run all over her naked body, 'before, behind, between, above, below'. Donne's poem is about discovery and conquest - the female body is memorably imagined as new virginal territory in an extended metaphor, or conceit. Delightedly the poet calls the woman 'Oh my America! My new-found land' and his 'Empire', and refers to her as a 'mine' from which he may extricate 'precious stones'. Rather racy material for a poet who would much later in life become the Dean of St Pauls' Cathedral.

Roberts recycles some of Donne's images, such as the references to a new-found land, to roving hands, to stripping for bed, to America and to mystic books. These connections highlight the dialogic nature of the latter poem, but are less significant than the conceit Roberts lifts and interrogates of the body as land. The modern poet also makes some important changes. Notably, for example, Donne's poem is addressed to his beloved, whereas Roberts' is addressed to Donne. Also *To his Mistress Going to Bed* is a seduction poem, a particular sub-class of love poem, whereas Roberts' poem is more mediative - if it is about love it is love in more abstract sense, not for a particular woman, but for humanity as a whole. Roberts also introduces scientific language at the end of the poem, arranged in a sort of litany. Although such language is absent from Donne's poem he is famous for his wide-ranging imagery and, in particular, his use of images drawn from the emerging seventeenth century science of cartography.

To his Mistress Going to Bed is written in a characteristically rough and vigorous iambic pentamenter and forms one solid, relentless block of persuasive text, with no space for uncertainty or right of reply. Donne's use of couplets creates momentum and, sonically, it is never long before one rhyme is united with its matching pair. Less overtly rhetorical, *To John Donne* is written without a regular metre to thrust the lines forward. Moreover Roberts shortens the lines, making them seem more tentative and hesitant than Donne's and he stretches the poem out, so that it looks more fragile on the page, like a string of words, or perhaps a strand of DNA. Robers also drops the vigorous couplet end rhymes, favouring instead more subtle and delicate occasional internal echoing, suggesting internal connections and resonances. And the tercet stanza form implies that there are more than two people in this story. In all these ways, in terms of diction, imagery and form Roberts' poem is both a homage to Donne and also a critique of his poem.

Map of the body

Donne's poem anticipates the discovery and exploration of the beloved's body as if in were a piece of terrain. In Roberts' poem this appropriating  process is already complete, the body has 'already been mapped', 'paced' and 'sized' up. The process is presented as being invasive and exposing; the body has been 'laid bare'. It is also a passionless and potentially exploitative process, entirely devoid of the erotic thrill of Donne's poem. If there is desire here, it is for knowledge and control. Mapping the body establishes this control; the details of the body are 'written down' so that predictions about its future can be calculated. Nowhere in this process is there any sense of the live human being whose body is the subject. Nor is there any indication that consent was granted or, indeed, even requested. Whereas Donne issues bold imperatives, 'unpin that spangled breastplate'; 'now off with those shoes', the anonymous and invisible agents mapping the body have no need to even communicate with their subject.

The colder, more scientific treatment of the body as an object culminates in a line that flatly contradicts Donne's metaphor of the female form as a 'mystic book'. Instead, now it has become simply, bleakly, a 'textbook of disease'. The body has not, however, only been mapped and mastered by 'medics' and charted on 'laptops', it has been colonised by far more invidious agents driven not by the search for knowledge but by the lure of the quick buck. Commodified and commercialised, the body's parts have been patented and the whole thing turned into property, 'carved up into real estate'. In the context of a human body that verb is particularly disturbing. And the subject herself has lost any control or say in this process to the extent that she is exiled from herself - she no longer owns her own body, 'she's no landowner'. Up until this point in the poem Donne has been addressed as an onlooker on this process. Now Roberts' makes his implications clear; it is not just this woman's body that has been conquered, colonised and commercialised, but all human bodies, all of our bodies, including Donne's have been subject to the same exploitation: The bankers have bought 'a piece of her and you'. And, just in case we weren't suitably alarmed by how quickly this process has escalated Roberts' hits us hard. The body has been turned into: 'ranches ringed with barbed wire / lights and guns' with signs shouting, 'KEEP OUT / OUR DOGS EAT TRESPASSERS'.

Arcadia not America

It's something of a surprise after this apocalyptic warning that the poem ends by shrinking the perspective back to the intimate, to the two lovers in an

gently erotic, pastoral, early summer, timeless scene, full of 'crab apples', 'silver birch', 'collar doves', 'greenfinches' and 'blossom'. This gentle, very English space is,  of course, the polar opposite to the previous nightmarish landscape. This is a space of mutuality, of things existing harmoniously with each other. The lovers 'seek each other out', are 'so close' to the apples and 'akin' to the grass; nature 'interweaves' with itself, enfolding the humans within its embrace, and all living things share a similar genetic code, a 'secret name'. Thus Roberts shows us that we can still find the sort of paradise Donne imagined on earth through mutual love. It seems, however, that we can only do this if we shut our eyes to the troubling wider context of what is actually going on in the world.

However, in a final, optimistic flourish, moving for the first time into imperative mode, Roberts imagines this loving scenario into an act not of selfish escapism or the expression of lust, as Donne had done, but of defiance, recovery and re-occupation of our bodies and our humanity by love: 'love's mass trespass' is to set out in order to 'claim back' our bodies. Turning the bodies 'co-ordinates' into a litany tops off and enacts this sense of reclamation.

John Donne crunched:

STRIPS – ALREADY – CRACKED – PACED – SIZED – PROBABILITY – LAPTOPS – MASTERED – HER – STARS – ATLAS – DISEASE – DUST – SETS – PATH – ROVING – LANDOWNER – LAW – PATENT – BANKERS – BOUGHT – AMERICA – WILDERNESS – ESTATE – WIRE – GUNS – TRESPASSERS – CARE – MAY – SEEK – SECRET – YOUR – APPLE – INTERWEAVE – AKIN – BLOSOM – LET – TRESPASS – CLAIM – BODIES – IS – LITANY

Wendy Cope, *After the Lunch*

Drama, trivia and confession

Why might someone, anyone, be afraid of falling in love? Celebrity magazines have a field day announcing who's partnered up with who, and rom-coms usually conclude with a breath-taking demonstration of love. In light of this, it's fair to say that falling in love has a certain amount of drama associated with it – and what if you're a shy introvert? Falling in love also brings with it a great deal of vulnerability. After all, a person's powerful feelings might not be reciprocated. Likewise, falling in love might not happen in the right place or at the right time, or with the right person! As this analysis will show, Wendy Cope adds to these thoughts and fears on falling in love.

Let's take the poem's title as a starting point. Why is it not simply 'After Lunch' or 'After a Lunch', but **After the Lunch**? Using the definite article ['the'] indicates that this was not any old lunch, but a momentous event. The

fact that the poem begins 'On Waterloo Bridge' pursues this rather serious tone. After all, bridges in London are cultural icons – not only for tourists, but also settings for meaningful 0observations and encounters. William Wordsworth's poem, *Composed Upon Westminster Bridge*, for example, depicts the beauty of London before its inhabitants have woken up. Waterloo Bridge is also the setting, and the title, of a popular romance film made in 1940 in which the bridge is crucial to the meeting of two lovers.

So what kind of momentous event does Cope represent?

'On Waterloo Bridge, where we said our goodbyes
the weather conditions bring tears to my eyes.
I wipe them away with a black woolly glove
and try not to notice I've fallen in love'

The fact these details are delivered by a first-person 'I' lends a certain confessional quality to this poem. This creates an intimacy with the reader, whilst also anticipating instances of self-dialogue that we'll discuss later on. Cope's language shifts from the significant – 'goodbyes' – to the commonplace and seemingly banal – 'weather conditions'. Given the way the poem sets itself up in a rather sincere manner, the latter phrase appears more suitable for television forecasters. Why doesn't Cope refer more lyrically to high winds or cold blasts? As it happens, this prosaic diction, or style of speech, deliberately undercuts the gravitas of the poem's opening. This happens again in the final line of the quatrain [or four-line stanza] through another juxtaposition of the trivial with the dramatic. We try not to notice a fly buzzing around the room, or someone speaking in the library as we're trying to read, but here the speaker tries not to notice that they've fallen in love! This change of scale – from the unimportant to a suddenly significant occurrence – comes as a surprise. It also encourages us to reconsider those 'tears' earlier in the stanza. Indeed, looking back it seems 'the weather conditions' might have just been an excuse, a cover up, for the embarrassment of crying.

But why has Cope decided to juxtapose the trivial with the dramatic in this confession –'[I] try not to notice I've fallen in love'? 'Try not to notice' underplays the event, and if we weren't reading carefully, we might skip over the line's key detail. This diminishment of what might otherwise be a life-changing experience continues more overtly in the second stanza:

'I am trying to think:
This is nothing. You're high on the charm and the drink'

Rather than the feeling of helplessness associated with 'falling' in love, it's clear that the speaker wants to remain in control. Cope's italicisation of text indicates the speaker's inner-dialogue. The speaker is not simply thinking 'This is nothing', but 'trying' to think 'This is nothing' as if it were a mantra that might be believed if repeated enough times. Unlike the lightly punctuated and mostly end-punctuated previous lines, the full stop that comes so early in the line warrants attention. The caesura, or pause, generated by the full stop makes 'This is nothing' a short, sharp declaration to be taken seriously. The following brief sentence explains the inconsequential nature of the feelings previously expressed: that the speaker has been charmed by their lunch-date and that alcohol may well have played a part in influencing their state of mind.

However, this attempt to control and explain away important emotions doesn't last long: The conjunction, 'But' signals a turn in the opposite direction. Cope creates a metaphor in writing of 'the juke-box inside me'. The juke-box appears to represent the speaker's heart that is 'playing a song' – perhaps a love long. This juke-box heart is associated with the speaker's instinct: the song the juke-box plays 'says something different' than what the speaker is trying, rationally, to tell themself. Whilst the juke-box is an apt metaphor for thinking about love and the inner-voice, looking up the word's  etymology adds to our interpretation. Indeed, 'juke', from West African origin, means 'disorderly'. Consequently, the juke-box emphasises the desire to surrender control and submit to the passionate, untamed inner-self. Cope emphasises the importance of listening to the inner-voice by asking 'And when was it wrong?' As a hypothetical question, we are led to believe the heart is fail-proof in its decision-making. Once again, a caesura means that we pause on the word 'different'. This punctuation slows down the pace of the poem and implies a moment of composed reflection.

'With the wind in my hair'

Internal rhyme in the second stanza creates an important comparison: the previous assertion that 'This is nothing' is transformed by the end of the stanza into the song 'That says something different' [emphasis added]. With the acceptance that perhaps the speaker's initial thought – 'I've fallen in love' – is in fact correct, the poem's third and final stanza let loose:

'On Waterloo Bridge with the wind in my hair

I am tempted to skip. You're a fool. I don't care.'

In contrast to the first stanza in which the speaker wipes away their tears and makes excuses for them in order to give the impression that they're in control, the third stanza opens with the speaker wild and windblown. The speaker, with 'wind in my hair', might evoke the romantic figures of films and books – Cathy in Emily Brontë's Wuthering Heights – if it weren't for the line running on to a more childlike image of skipping. Italicisation of text once again indicates the speaker's self-dialogue, but this time the sceptical brain has little opportunity to hush the passionate heart. As Cope summarises 'The head does its best but the heart is the boss'. The alliteration of 'head' and 'heart', as well as 'best' and 'boss', brings their juxtaposition to the fore. Moreover, 'head and 'heart' are pararhymes as their vowels are different but both begin and end with the same consonants [this is almost true for 'best' and 'boss']. The way these words echo each other emphasise their jostle for the speaker's attention: in the previous two stanzas the head and the heart have been in competition, yet here, finally, the heart is named champion.

The fact that Cope explains 'I admit it before I am halfway across' indicates the speed at which the speaker is moving across the bridge: suggesting that following their heart wasn't such a hard decision to make after all. Furthermore, as Cope compares the pace of the speaker's judgement with the length of the bridge, the bridge takes on symbolic value. Bridges link us to different places and territories, and are often used figuratively to represent a connection, process or liminal state. Think for example of the common phrases 'bridge the divide' or 'Let's cross that bridge when we come to it'. Although the bridge is obviously a physical setting in the poem, the bridge also lends itself to the poem's event: the transition or journey of someone falling in love.

Looking back at the beginning of the poem we see just how vital this bridge is in Cope's poem. 'On Waterloo Bridge' is a refrain that begins each quatrain. But what's the reason for this anaphora, this repeated phrase at the start of these lines? We might return to our opening consideration of how bridges have been key settings in already existing literature and film. The bridge in Cope's poem is the location in which she realises she has fallen in love ~~and~~; by repeating this phrase it sticks in our mind and becomes memorable, iconic. Yet there's another way of looking at this anaphora. Our analysis has considered Cope's comparison of the head and the heart, reason and emotion, and this anaphora supports the speaker's deliberation between these forces. As the speaker frees themselves from their sensible, no-nonsense attitude, listens to the juke-box's song, and becomes 'tempted to skip', 'On Waterloo Bridge' is an orienting phrase. It suggests a certain amount of stability despite the speaker changing their mind twice during the poem. The speaker might self-deprecatingly speak of themselves as 'a fool', but Cope suggests they have not taken complete leave of their senses.

Slave to the rhythm

Having analysed the poem - looking at image and metaphor, diction, caesurae and anaphora – it is important to think about how these elements are carried by Cope's use of form and structure. One of the first things you might have noticed about the poem is its rhythm. Reading the poem out loud exemplifies the text's jaunty music. How is such a rhythm created? The answer is through 'anapestic tetrameter'. Let's unpack this technical term! An 'anapest' is a foot of three syllables: the main thing to remember here is that there are two short, or unstressed, syllables followed by a long stressed one.

Take this example of an anapest in which the text in bold represents the long syllable 'you're a fool'. Here's another: 'I don't care'. 'Tetrameter' means that there are four beats in the line, so here's a whole line of anapaestic tetrameter:

'I am tempted to skip. You're a fool. I don't care.'

Another example comes earlier in the poem:

'This is nothing. You're high on the charm and the drink.'

Not every line in Cope's poem is strict anapaestic tetrameter. Some lines begin with iambs, rather than anapests. Take, for example, 'On Waterloo Bridge' which has an iamb and then an anapest. This slight irregularity, however, does not detract from the rhythm of the poem. So what is the effect of anapaestic tetrameter? Having just considered the speed at which the speaker is moving across the bridge, Cope's use of anapaestic tetrameter emphasises rapidity. This is supported by the rhyming couplets throughout the poem: as the rhyme appears quickly we are led on to the next line and the next. Moreover, emphasising the contrast between head and heart, the formal patterning of the poem evokes the meticulous, self-conscious work of the brain [anapaestic tetrameter is pretty demanding!], whilst the light, skipping metre echoes the fluttering heart. What else might we say about the rhythm? What kind of feeling does it create? Partly due to its speed, the pattern of stresses in the lines create an upbeat and buoyant tempo. This upbeat quality in the opening lines initially seems contrary to the poem's melancholy tone as the speaker cries. Yet, this contrast echoes other contrasts previous discussed: the upbeat rhythm of the poem supports the distinction between the inconsequential and the dramatic diction in the speaker's trying 'not to notice I've fallen in love'. This contrast between buoyant rhythm and heartfelt revelation creates a humorous effect. Indeed, anapaestic tetrameter has long been associated with comic verse. Dr Seuss, for instance, showcases the potential for anapaestic tetrameter in his well-known, nonsensical narratives. Likewise, Lewis Carroll's *The Hunting of the Snark*. Certainly, later in the poem, Cope's bouncy rhythm emphasises the childlike quality of the newly carefree speaker as they are tempted to skip across the bridge. Cope's anapaestic tetrameter thus creates a sensitive, humorous and [towards the poem's conclusion] liberating backdrop to her speaker's eventful self-dialogue.

The comic quality of the poem is very much in keeping with other poems by Cope. Indeed, Cope is famous for writing popular 'light comic' verse that often punctures romantic sentimentality and literary pretension with wry, down-to-earth humour. A social ironist and formalist, she might be compared to John Betjeman or Philip Larkin, though Cope's work is gentler, more generous and less judgemental than Larkin's. The term 'light verse' is often used pejoratively to suggest a lack of substance and seriousness. Comprehensible, employing an ordinary vocabulary and everyday phrasing, free from linguistic grandiloquence, tidily organised and neatly rhymed, does After the Lunch lack seriousness or depth? I don't think so. The analysis has shown how the poem is carefully constructed at every level: from the juxtaposition of language and metaphor to the syntactical structure of lines and the poem's overall form.

You might have noticed that this analysis has referred to 'the speaker' and refrained from pronouns such as 'he' and 'she' to describe the 'I' in the

 poem. This has kept us focused upon the poem in front of us. However, how does reading the first-person 'I' as Wendy Cope make a difference? What if the poet is actually the speaker? Let's start by looking at when this poem was written. After the Lunch is collected in Serious Concerns, which was published in 2009 when Cope was in her sixties. Some investigative work into Cope's personal life shows that her relationship [now marriage] with poet Lachlan Mackinnon began when Cope was 49. To fall in love at this age is relatively late! So how is this significant to the poem? Well, as the opening paragraph to this essay suggested, falling in love is associated with celebrity magazines…rom coms…with youth! A mature adult is expected to be worldly wise and certainly not tempted to skip across the bridge like a little girl. In turn, thinking about the context of Cope's poem and reading it as if Cope were speaking herself gives us a more personal answer to the first question of this essay: of why someone, anyone, might be afraid of falling in love.

The Lunch Crunch

WATERLOO – CONDITIONS – WIPE – FALLEN – TRYING – NOTHING – JUKE-BOX – DIFFERENT – WIND – SKIP – HEART – ADMIT

A sonnet of revision activities

1. Reverse millionaire: 10,000 points if students can guess the poem just from one word from it. You can vary the difficulty as much as you like. For example, 'clams', would be fairly easily identifiable as from Sexton's poem whereas 'fleet' would be more difficult. 1000 points if students can name the poem from a single phrase or image – 'portion out the stars and dates'. 100 points for a single line. 10 points for recognising the poem from a stanza. Play individually or in teams.

2. Research the poet. Find one sentence about them that you think sheds light on their poem in the anthology. Compare with your classmates. Or find a couple more lines or a stanza by a poet and see if others can recognise the writer from their lines.

3. Write a cento based on one or more of the poems. A cento is a poem constructed from lines from other poems. Difficult, creative, but also fun, perhaps.

4. Read 3 or 4 other poems by one of the poets. Write a pastiche. See if classmates can recognise the poet you're imitating.

5. Write the introduction for a critical guide on the poems aimed at next year's yr. 12 class.

6. Practice comparing and contrasting: Write the name of each poem on a separate card. Turn face down and mix up the cards. Turn back over any three cards at random. What do two of the poems have in

common? How is the third one different? Replace the cards and do the exercise again.

7. Use the poet Glynn Maxwell's typology of poems to arrange the poems into different groups. In his excellent book, On Poetry, Maxwell suggests poems have four dominant aspects, which he calls solar, lunar, musical and visual. A solar poem hits home, is immediately striking. A lunar poem, by contrast, is more mysterious and might not give up its meanings so easily. Ideally a lunar poem will haunt your imagination. Written mainly for the ear, a musical poem focuses on the sounds of language, rather than the meanings. Think of Lewis Carroll's *Jabberwocky*. A visual poem is self-conscious about how it looks to the eye. Concrete poems are the ultimate visual poems. According to Maxwell the very best poems are strong in each dimension. Try applying this test to each poem. Which ones come out on top?

8. Maxwell also recommends conceptualising the context in which the words of the poem are created or spoken. Which poems would suit being read around a camp fire? Which would be better declaimed from the top of a tall building? Which might you imagine on a stage? Which ones are more like conversation overheard? Which are the easiest and which the most difficult to place?

9. Mr Maxwell is a fund of interesting ideas. He suggests all poems dramatise a battle between the forces of whiteness and blackness, nothingness and somethingness, sound and silence, life and death. In each poem what is the dynamic between whiteness and blackness? Which appears to have the upper hand?

10. Maxwell argues too that the whiteness is a different thing for different poems. Consider each poem's whiteness in the light of this idea. See any differences?

11. Still thinking in terms of evaluation, consider the winnowing effect of time. Which of these poems do you think might be still read in 20, a 100 or 200 years? Why?

12. Give yourself only the first and last line of one of the poems. Without peeking at the original, try to fill in the middle. Easy level: write in prose. Expert level: attempt verse.

13. According to Russian Formalist critics poetry performs a 'controlled explosion on ordinary language'. What evidence can you find in this selection of controlled linguistic detonations?

14. A famous musician once said that though he wasn't the best at playing all the notes, nobody played the silences better. In Japanese garden water features the sound of a water drop is designed to make us notice the silence around it. Try reading one of the poems in the light of these comments, focusing on the use of white space, caesuras, punctuation – all the devices that create the silence on which the noise of the poem rests.

15. In *Notes on the Art of Poetry*, Dylan Thomas wrote that 'the best craftmanship always leaves holes and gaps in the works of the poem so that something that is not in the poem can creep, crawl, flash or thunder in'. Examine a poem in the light of this comment, looking for

its holes and gaps. If you discover these, what 'creeps', 'crawls' or 'flashes' in to fill them?

16. Different types of poems conceive the purpose of poetry differently. Broadly speaking Augustan poets of the eighteenth century aimed to impress their readers with the wit of their ideas and the elegance of the expression. In contrast, Romantic poets wished to move their readers' hearts. Characteristically Victorian poets aimed to teach the readers some kind of moral principle or example. Self-involved, avant-garde Modernists weren't overly bothered about finding, never mind pleasing, a general audience. What impact do the AQA anthology poems seek to have? Do they seek to amuse, appeal to the heart, teach us something? Are they like soliloquies – the overheard inner workings of thinking – or more like speeches or mini-plays? Try placing each poem somewhere on the following continuums. Then create a few continuums of your own. As ever, comparison with your classmates will prove illuminating.

Emotional..intellectual

Feelings...ideas

Internal...external

Contemplative...rhetorical

Open..guarded

NB
Yes, we know. This is that rare old bird, a sixteen-line sonnet, following the example of the poet George Meredith, no less.

Critical soundbites

In this demanding revision activity, students have to match the following excerpts from criticism to the poet whose work they describe. [Answers are at the end of this book]. In an added twist for this second volume, some of the sound bites come from the poets themselves...

1. 'A deeply felt hurt is laid down as ground-swell to counterpoint the verbal game-playing that takes place on the wavelengths above.'

2. 'Noted especially for their out-spoken politics,' this poet 'treats issues of class, race and power with extraordinary formal brilliance and technique.'

3. Their 'poetry is known for its aural beauty and finely-wrought textures. Often described as a regional poet,' they are 'also a traditionalist who deliberately gestures back towards the "pre-modern" worlds.

4. 'The traumatic issues' this poet 'grappled with during their childhood — death, mental illness, loneliness, and disillusionment — became themes in their poetry and stories.'

5. 'They are an important poet not only because of their courage in dealing with previously forbidden subjects, but because they can make the language sing.'

6. 'Their poetry demonstrates the scrupulous awareness of someone who refuses to be taken in by inflated notions of either art or life.'

7. 'The unassuming technical craft of their poetry and its emotional restraint are qualities that were praised by the poets and critics of the period and continued to be abiding characteristics of their work. An important theme is their Catholicism and many of their poems have a devotional aspect.'

8. 'From first to last, their own work reflects a melancholy skepticism too honest to give final assent to any fixed system. They might sympathize with, and even envy, those who believed, but they remained a detached outsider.'

9. 'A lyric poet with philosophical and metaphysical concerns... [with a] skill at rooting the miraculous in the everyday.'

10. This poet's 'themes include language and the representation of reality; the construction of the self; gender issues; contemporary culture; and many different forms of alienation, oppression and social inequality. [they write] in everyday, conversational language, making their poems appear deceptively simple.'

11. 'Taking his symbols from the public domain,' this poet 'developed, as many critics note, an original, modern idiom and a sense of directness and economy.'

12. This poet expressed their 'mind freely in the best American tradition, upholding freedom and individualism; championing radical, idealistic humanist tenets; and holding broad sympathies and a deep reverence for life.'

13. 'The humour and knowingness' of this poet, 'is, at times, also offset with poignancy... [their] poems demonstrate an awareness of the outsider, which is in keeping with the undeclared premise of being accessible to a wider readership.'

14. 'Sincere, honest, emotionally reticent, descriptively precise, detached but compassionate, unpretentious. There is no self pity, in this poet's verse and very little that is melodramatic.'

Comparing the poems

Only at A-level is there a requirement to compare these poems. As we indicated in the introduction, the best comparisons arise from choosing texts that have strong differences as well as similarities. Texts that are too similar or too different make the task much more difficult. Although these poems obviously share the broad theme of love, as we've discovered, they explore very different types of love and approach the topic in a wide range of ways.

In the exam you'll be asked to compare at least two poems with a prose text, specifically a novel. It's vital that in this mixed genre type task that you keep the poetic elements of the poetry to the fore, such as sonic imagery and stanza form, in order to show that you understand the different nature of poems and novels. Broadly in your comparison you will need to explore ideas, feelings and effects and the techniques used to generate these. Of course, there are many ways in which the poems could be grouped. And we might recall Paul Muldoon's 'fruitful misalliances'. What follows are only a few suggestions to get you thinking, arguing and making informed decisions for yourself.

Millay's *I, Being Born a Woman* is a sonnet, that most conventional form for a love poem, as is *Timer* by Harrison. Millay's poem dramatises the head's attempts to rule the heart and could be compared to the curtal sonnet, *Wild Oats*, by Larkin which also deals with love, or at least lust, rejected. Both Millay and Larkin are far too steely-eyed for any giddy ideas about romance. Like Sexton's *For my Lover* and Mew's *A Quoi Bon Dire* Millay's sonnet can also be read through the prism of feminism; all three poems express rejections of the various impositions placed on women by patriarchal societies.

Heaney's *Punishment*, Douglas' *Vergissmeinnicht* and Frost's *Love & a Question* explore conflicts between different types of love and different loyalties. Frost's poem also features a love triangle, as does Sexton's *For my Lover*. Whereas Frost's approach is elliptical, nudging the reader in the right direction, and his style homely, Sexton is rather more demonstrative and unsettling.

One Flesh and *Talking in Bed* make a good pair. Both concern love cooling off in intimate, domestic settings and both writers express themselves in a semi-detached and understated style. This style also brings Harrison's *Timer* to mind, which, like *One Flesh* is a poem about love between, and for, parents. Like *Wild Oats* and *Vergissmeinnicht* these poems also explore candidly the lack of appropriate or expected feelings.

Two of the more conventionally romantic and celebratory poems in the selection, *Meeting Point* and *After the Lunch* present that transports of love. Both poems feature couples in love, but where MacNeice semi-detaches himself through the third person perspective Cope braves the more exposing first person point of view.

Duffy's *The Love Poem* and Roberts' *To John Donne* are the most obviously intertextual of these poems. Both are in dialogue with previous writers, but whereas Roberts addresses a speaker writer and a specific poem as a way into exploring genetic decoding, Duffy's poem is more self-reflective and pugnaciously challenges the whole [male] literary canon of love poetry. In this feminist sense, Duffy's poem could be compared with any of the other poems by women in the anthology.

Which leaves us one last poem. That curious fish, *Long Finish*. It could be compared with Heaney's poem because it deals, albeit more obliquely, with The Troubles in Northern Ireland. And Heaney and Muldoon are, of course, Irish poets in an English exam board anthology, as, also of course, is MacNeice. The surprising elements Muldoon includes in his love poem might recall Larkin's dogged unromanticism in *Wild Oats*. Or if we consider the way Muldoon adapts the traditional form of the ballade [that bastard son of a etc. etc.] we might compare that again with Larkin's truncating of the sonnet form in *Wild Oats*, Harrison's elongation of it in *Timer*, or with Heaney's innovative use of the Petrarchan lover's blazon.

Glossary

ALLITERATION – the repetition of consonants at the start of neighbouring words in a line

ANAPAEST - a three beat pattern of syllables, unstress, unstress, stress. E.g. 'on the moon', 'to the coast', 'anapaest'

ANTITHESIS - the use of balanced opposites

APOSTROPHE – a figure of speech addressing a person, object or idea

ASSONANCE – vowel rhyme, e.g. sod and block

BLANK VERSE – unrhymed lines of iambic pentameter

BLAZON – a male lover describing the parts of his beloved

CADENCE – the rise of fall of sounds in a line of poetry

CAESURA – a distinct break in a poetic line, usually marked by punctuation

COMPLAINT – a type of love poem concerned with loss and mourning

CONCEIT – an extended metaphor

CONSONANCE – rhyme based on consonants only, e.g. book and back

COUPLET – a two line stanza, conventionally rhyming

DACTYL – the reverse pattern to the anapaest; stress, unstress, unstress. E.g. 'Strong as a'

DRAMATIC MONOLOGUE – a poem written in the voice of a distinct character

ELEGY – a poem in mourning for someone dead

END-RHYME – rhyming words at the end of a line

END-STOPPED – the opposite of enjambment; i.e. when the sentence and the poetic line stop at the same point

ENJAMBMENT – where sentences run over the end of lines and stanzas

FIGURATIVE LANGUAGE – language that is not literal, but employs figures of speech, such as metaphor, simile and personification

FEMININE RHYME – a rhyme that ends with an unstressed syllable or unstressed syllables.

FREE VERSE – poetry without metre or a regular, set form

GOTHIC – a style of literature characterised by psychological horror, dark deeds and uncanny events

HEROIC COUPLETS – pairs of rhymed lines in iambic pentameter

HYPERBOLE – extreme exaggeration

IAMBIC – a metrical pattern of a weak followed by a strong stress, ti-TUM, like a heart beat

IMAGERY – the umbrella term for description in poetry. Sensory imagery refers to descriptions that appeal to sight, sound and so forth; figurative imagery refers to the use of devices such as metaphor, simile and personification

JUXTAPOSITION – two things placed together to create a strong contrast

LYRIC – an emotional, personal poem usually with a first person speaker

MASCULINE RHYME – an end rhyme on a strong syllable

METAPHOR – an implicit comparison in which one thing is said to be another

METAPHYSICAL – a type of poetry characterised by wit and extended metaphors

METRE – the regular pattern organising sound and rhythm in a poem

MOTIF – a repeated image or pattern of language, often carrying thematic significance

OCTET OR OCTAVE – the opening eight lines of a sonnet

ONOMATOPOEIA – bang, crash, wallop

PENTAMETER – a poetic line consisting of five beats

PERSONIFICATION – giving human characteristics to inanimate things

PLOSIVE – a type of alliteration using 'p' and 'b' sounds

QUATRAIN – a four-line stanza

REFRAIN – a line or lines repeated like a chorus

ROMANTIC – A type of poetry characterised by a love of nature, by strong emotion and heightened tone

SESTET – the last six lines in a sonnet

SIMILE – an explicit comparison of two different things

SONNET – a form of poetry with fourteen lines and a variety of possible set rhyme patterns

SPONDEE – two strong stresses together in a line of poetry

STANZA – the technical name for a verse

SYMBOL – something that stands in for something else. Often a concrete representation of an idea.

SYNTAX – the word order in a sentence. doesn't Without sense English syntax make. Syntax is crucial to sense: For example, though it uses all the same words, 'the man eats the fish' is not the same as 'the fish eats the man'

TERCET – a three-line stanza

TETRAMETER – a line of poetry consisting of four beats

TROCHEE – the opposite of an iamb; stress, unstress, strong, weak.

VILLANELLE – a complex interlocking verse form in which lines are recycled

VOLTA – the 'turn' in a sonnet from the octave to the sestet

Recommended reading

For the committed reader there's a brilliant overview of developments in English poetry in Part 2 of The Oxford English Literary History, volume 12, by Randall Stevenson.

More general books on writing, reading & analysing poetry:

Atherton, C. & Green, A. Teaching English Literature 16-19. NATE, 2013

Bate, J. Ted Hughes, The Unauthorised Life. William Collins, 2016

Bowen et al. The Art of Poetry, vol.1-4. Peripeteia Press, 2015-16

Brinton, I. Contemporary Poetry. CUP, 2009

Eagleton, T. How to Read a Poem. Wiley & Sons, 2006

Fry, S. The Ode Less Travelled. Arrow, 2007

Hamilton, I. & Noel-Todd, J. Oxford Companion to Modern Poetry, OUP, 2014

Heaney, S. The Government of the Tongue. Farrar, Straus & Giroux, 1976

Herbert, W. & Hollis, M. Strong Words. Bloodaxe, 2000

Howarth, P. The Cambridge Introduction to Modernist Poetry. CUP, 2012

Hurley, M. & O'Neill, M. Poetic Form, An Introduction. CUP, 2012

Meally, M. & Bowen, N. The Art of Writing English Literature Essays, Peripeteia Press, 2014

Maxwell, G. On Poetry. Oberon Masters, 2012

Padel, R. 52 Ways of Looking at a Poem. Vintage, 2004

Padel, R. The Poem and the Journey. Vintage, 2008

Paulin, T. The Secret Life of Poems. Faber & Faber, 2011

Quinn, J. The Cambridge Introduction to Modern Irish Poetry, CUP, 2008

Schmidt, M. Lives of the Poets, Orion, 1998

Wolosky, S. The Art of Poetry: How to Read a Poem. OUP, 2008.

About the authors

Dr Carol Atherton is an experienced Head of English with a first class degree from Oxford University. The author of *Defining Literary Criticism: Scholarship, Authority and the Possession of Literary Knowledge* and co-author of *Teaching English Literature 16-19* [Routledge, 2013], Carol is a fellow of the English Association.

Head of English and freelance writer, Neil Bowen has a Masters Degree in Literature & Education from Cambridge University and is a member of Ofqual's experts panel for English. He is the author of *The Art of Writing English Essays for GCSE*, co-author of *The Art of Writing English Essays for A-level and Beyond* and of *The Art of Poetry*, volumes 1-5. Neil runs the peripeteia project, bridging the gap between A-level and degree level English courses: www.peripeteia.webs.com.

James Browning was awarded a double first degree in English Literature by the University of Cambridge. His particular interest at uni. was 20th century Anglo-American poetry and he wrote dissertations on the New York School poet, Frank O'Hara, on Dylan Thomas, and T. S. Eliot. He is currently a private tutor and is working on his writing.

Isabel Galleymore received her doctorate in contemporary ecopoetics and metaphor from the University of Exeter. Her articles have featured in the Journal of Ecocriticism and Green Letters, and her debut pamphlet of poems, *Dazzle Ship*, was published by Worple Press. Winner of the Basil Bunting Award and Jane Martin Poetry Prize, she is currently preparing for a writing residency in the Peruvian Amazon.

YiWen Hon studied English Literature at Uuniversity College London from where she graduated with a First. Since then YiWen has completed her Masters degree and worked as an academic librarian.

Head of A-level English, Michael Meally, holds an MA in American Literature as well as degrees in English Literature and Engineering. Michael's literary interests include detective/crime fiction, postcolonial literature and Greek tragedy. He is the co-author of *The Art of Writing English Literature Essays for A-level and Beyond* and *The Art of Poetry, volumes 1-5*. Michael writes regularly for the English & Media Centre magazine.

Answers to critical soundbites:

1. Muldoon
2. Harrison
3. Heaney
4. Mew
5. Sexton
6. Larkin
7. Jennings
8. MacNeice
9. Roberts
10. Duffy
11. Frost
12. Millay
13. Cope
14. Douglas

A final revision task: Students create their own anonymised critical sound bites. The class have to match the sound bite to the poet/ poem.

Critical sound bites adapted from:

The Cambridge Introduction to Modern Irish Poetry, 1800-200

https://literature.britishcouncil.org

http://www.warpoets.org/

http://www.poetryfoundation.org

http://www.theguardian.com

Printed in Great Britain
by Amazon